NORTH OF THE

Master Solvers'Club

The following pieces first appeared in *The Kibitzer*: An Old Approach, To the Editor, Dear Partner, Live by the Sword, Team Match, Two Bridge Tales, So Long Dad, The Man from La Mancha; we are grateful to the Vine family for permission to reprint them here. All others are © *The Bridge World*, and are reproduced here by permission.

Master Point Press   Website: http://www.masterpointpress.com
331 Douglas Ave.   Email: info@masterpointpress.com
Toronto, Ontario, Canada   (416) 781-0351
M5M 1H2

Library and Archives Canada Cataloguing in Publication
Vine, Frank
      North of the Master solvers' club : the bridge writings of Frank Vine / written by Frank Vine.
ISBN 978-1-897106-40-2
      1. Contract bridge. I. Title.
GV1282.3.V55 2008   795.41'5   C2008-904159-3

We acknowledge the financial support of the Government of Canada through the Book Publishing Industry Development Program (BPIDP) for our publishing activities.

Editor	Ray Lee
Copy editing	Sarah Howden
Interior format	Sarah Howden
Cover and interior design	Olena S. Sullivan/New Mediatrix
Cover photo	Ronald

Printed in Canada
1 2 3 4 5 6 7   12 11 10 09 08

TABLE OF CONTENTS

FOREWORD

The only thing my father liked better than a good bridge game was a good bridge story. Growing up as children of two avid bridge players, my brother and sister and I were often bewildered at the discussion of major and minor suits, Gerber and Stayman. Most astonishing to us was the way our parents remembered bridge hands in detail years after they had been played. It was a long time before we understood what they were talking about but we still learned a lot from these discussions. We learned geography (and the best places to eat) from their tales of bridge tournaments across the continent; we learned that games can keep the mind sharp; and most importantly, we learned a kind of democracy. Our home was filled with bridge players from every walk of life. Income, profession, race or religion was of no consequence — all that mattered was their shared love of the game of bridge.

My parents spent many happy evenings at the local bridge club. In those bygone days, though, the hours in the late afternoon belonged to men who dropped in to play for a few hours after work. My brother, Ron, recalls that when he was ten years old he was driving with my mother one day when she happened to pass by the bridge club and noticed my father's car parked outside. Perhaps to make a point, she sent my little brother into the club by himself to remind my father that dinner was waiting at home. Ron remembers walking into that strange place for the first time. The room was dim in the early twilight and, as was common in those days, filled with the haze of cigarette smoke. Rows of men sat at tables intently studying their cards. Suddenly the phone rang, and as the director of the club reached for the phone Ron heard five voices say in unison, "If that's my wife — I'm not here!"

Humor is another thing we learned to associate with bridge. Many times my father returned from a tournament with a funny tale or unusual story. Once he was seated against a young couple who were playing their very first hand at their very first bridge tournament. In the middle of the hand the husband piped up, "Convention!" "Yes," my father replied, eager to see what obscure convention the couple had uncovered. "When I go like this," the young man said, tugging his earlobe, "it means I have three aces."

Since the convention had been announced to everyone, my father decided that it was okay with him.

Most of the amusing incidents that happened to my father at the bridge table made their way into his stories. I hope you enjoy them.

Ira Vine

EDITOR'S INTRODUCTION

It is more than twenty years since Frank Vine passed away at the early age of fifty, and he was far too good a bridge writer to be allowed to fade away into obscurity.

Frank made his living as an attorney in Hamilton, Ontario, a steel-industry town overshadowed by its more glamorous neighbor, Toronto. He was one of a number of Hamiltonians who regularly traveled to the big tournaments in Toronto and beyond, and who were regularly successful. The pinnacle of his playing career came in 1969, when he won the National Men's Pairs — undoubtedly the strongest pairs event on the North American bridge calendar at the time, but sadly today no longer held, a victim of political correctness. Frank's partner in that event, Mike Martino (another Hamilton lawyer), was also to die very young. Frank and his wife Lillian were well known on the local tournament trail, and when my wife Linda and I began playing bridge together in the 1970s, we frequently encountered the Vines as opponents.

Frank was a tough competitor, and his acerbic wit tended to make him as many enemies as friends. However, it is Frank Vine the writer that we celebrate in this book, and it was in his writing that his dry sense of humor and ability to skewer the pompous and ridiculous came into their own. Frank contributed articles, letters and editorials to bridge publications far and wide, from the local *Kibitzer* to the *ACBL Bulletin* and the prestigious *Bridge World*. It is perhaps as a *Bridge World* writer that he was best known. For more than fifteen years, he regularly entertained readers with satire, parody, and trenchant comments on the bridge scene. He was twice invited to appear as a guest Editorial writer, an honor that few receive even once.

Frank Vine's writing seems to fall naturally into three categories, so that is the way this book is organized. First, the Cornelius Coldbottom stories, whose central character is reminiscent of David Silver's *alter ego*, Professor Silver. Like Silver, Vine uses his protagonist to poke fun at bridge players' foibles and shortcomings, and even at some serious issues of ethics, propriety and the laws. Coldbottom, the sage of the Wentworth Bridge and Social Club, dispenses advice to lesser mortals, slices of bridge philosophy that seem to work when he applies them, but not when others do. And on one glorious occasion, he even manages to get the better of Wentworth's nemesis, the Blue Team from Stoney Creek.

Comprising the second section, presented with Frank's usual wit and polish, is a group of pieces we have gathered together under the heading of

"Comment". These are representative of Frank's views on how the game should be played, and his observations on the people he encountered while doing so. Written more than twenty years ago, they seem as fresh and applicable to the modern game as they were at the time they first appeared.

Finally we return to fiction with a third section that we have entitled "Parody". Here you will find bridge versions of literary masterpieces (my favorite is *Rashomon*, where the same deal is described four times, from the point of view of each player) alongside brilliant send-ups of favorite *Bridge World* features such as "Master Solvers' Club" and "You be the Judge".

The Bridge World published the proverbial slim volume of Frank Vine's material a few years ago, but it has been unavailable now for some time. This Master Point Press anthology has been published with the permission of Frank's family and of the Editor of *The Bridge World*, Jeff Rubens. John Carruthers, the current Editor of the *Kibitzer*, was also immensely helpful in gathering material for us, as was Tom Dawson, whose comprehensive collection of bridge magazines was, as always, an invaluable resource. This book would not have been possible without their help and support.

If you are old enough to remember Frank's work, we hope you will be pleased to have this more comprehensive collection to allow you to redis- cover your old favorites. If you are young enough not to have encountered Frank Vine before, you have a treat in store.

Ray Lee
Editor
October 2008

THE
Coldbottom Chronicles

CORNELIUS COLDBOTTOM ON DECEPTION

> *Modern players may well miss the passing reference to a Consolation event, which in context is very funny. Back in the day, an Open Pairs event always consisted of two sessions, the first of which was labeled "Qualifying". After this, the top half of the field continued into the Final, with some carryover, while the rest started over from scratch in the one-session Consolation — often referred to as "The Swamp". Those who went on to play the evening session in the Swamp often did so after drowning their sorrows over dinner — with the result that scores in the Swamp could be more or less random. I remember playing in the Swamp at a Sectional many years ago, and not bothering to stay for the scores, estimating our game at 40% or thereabouts. Indeed, my partner and I retired to the bar and entertained our friends with tales of the ludicrous things we had done to produce such a bad game. It wasn't until the next day we discovered we had won the event.*

"When you come right down to it, there are only two kinds of bridge players. The majority are what I call card pushers. Many of them, having studied long and diligently, are quite competent. They are familiar with all the latest squeezes and smother plays. In addition, they know that if such and so are divided such and so, the play of the queen will win 2.34% more often than laying down the ace. The only thing they lack is inspiration. Then, of course, there are those who hear voices."

The speaker was Professor Cornelius Coldbottom, leading bridge authority of the Wentworth County Bridge and Social Club. The place was North Caledonia on the final day of Bridge Week, between sessions of the Open Pairs. His audience: the contingent that had traveled down from Hamilton in an effort to win for our club the most prized bridge laurel of Southern Ontario, the famous Chicken Roost Trophy.

"Those who hear voices," he continued, "are few in number, and are rarely found among the winners at tournament time. That is because they disdain the game of average plus, and the less than one-and-one-half mistakes per session approach. They seek glory instead in the triumph of guile, the swing created out of thin air.

"Theirs, of course, is not a science, but an art. Nevertheless, there are certain sound principles, which can be learned and applied. Let me illustrate by examining some of the hands from this afternoon's session."

The first board Professor Coldbottom discussed was #7. I was surprised. Although my score had been below average, I could see no way in which it might have been improved.

Dealer South
Both vulnerable

```
              ♠ K Q 2
              ♡ 10
              ◊ A Q J 5 4
              ♣ J 9 8 7
  ♠ J 10 9        N        ♠ 8 7 6 5
  ♡ A K 3 2    W     E     ♡ 6 5 4
  ◊ 6 3 2         S        ◊ 9 8 7
  ♣ A 6 5                  ♣ K 4 3
              ♠ A 4 3
              ♡ Q J 9 8 7
              ◊ K 10
              ♣ Q 10 2
```

WEST	NORTH	EAST	SOUTH
			1♡
pass	2◊	pass	2NT
pass	3NT	all pass	

West led the jack of spades. I had a sure nine tricks. If I could establish the hearts before the opponents cashed their ace-king of clubs, I would make eleven tricks. Deceptively, I won the king of spades in dummy and led the ten of hearts. West won his king and led another spade. I took this in my hand with the ace and led the queen of hearts. West captured this with his ace, and I pitched a club from dummy. I could see his lips moving as he counted my blessings. Finally he laid down the ace of clubs and it was all over. Three notrump on the nose.

"The principle at work here is that of diminishing greed," said Professor Coldbottom. "Declarer was greedy for eleven tricks but West was greedy for nine. He was able to look into declarer's heart and guess what he was doing. Since it was exactly what he would have done had he been in declarer's place, it fell, as we say in the trade, well within his experience."

"I too was greedy, but only for ten tricks. Accordingly, I played as you all did to the first three tricks, except that on the queen of hearts I discarded from dummy not a club but a small diamond. West put himself in my shoes and immediately credited his partner with the king of diamonds. For what kind of normal greedy declarer would pitch away from a sure five tricks in dummy? He returned a spade, knowing that partner would get in with the king of diamonds to cash the long spade. If clubs were coming, they could come later. It was, as you see, later than he thought."

The next deal that led to discussion was #5. Again one of my own, and one that I felt I had handled to perfection.

Dealer East
East-West vulnerable

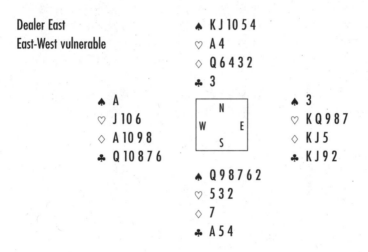

♠ K J 10 5 4
♡ A 4
◇ Q 6 4 3 2
♣ 3

♠ A   ♠ 3
♡ J 10 6   ♡ K Q 9 8 7
◇ A 10 9 8   ◇ K J 5
♣ Q 10 8 7 6   ♣ K J 9 2

♠ Q 9 8 7 6 2
♡ 5 3 2
◇ 7
♣ A 5 4

WEST	NORTH	EAST	SOUTH
		1♡	pass
2♣	2NT	3♣	4♠
5♡	all pass		

With a club lead and a ruff the hand was down one. West chose game in hearts as they were playing five-card majors. Had he decided to play in clubs, we would have had to maneuver a diamond ruff in order to beat it — a difficult defense which I was just as happy not to have to find. In practice, a plus score was well above average, although, as you can see, four spades is unbeatable.

"The principle to be used in hands of this nature," said Professor Coldbottom, "has been enunciated by some of my colleagues under the heading of advanced canapé.

"At my table the bidding was the same until East's three clubs. I then introduced three *diamonds*. West had to choose between game and penalty, and opted for game, bidding three notrump."

"Two down on a spade lead," I muttered admiringly. "Did your partner lead a spade?"

"I did not travel all the way to Caledonia to defend three notrump with a hand like this," said Professor Coldbottom witheringly. "When it came around to me again I bid four diamonds. This time West chose the penalty, doubling in a loud uncultured tone. I removed this to four spades.

"By this time West had it all figured out. On the bidding his partner was marked with at most one diamond, and with a lot of spades. He would double and lead the ace and another diamond. The penalty might even exceed nine hundred points. As you can see, the penalty was exactly 690." The final exhibit was deal #20. Again my bidding came up for discussion.

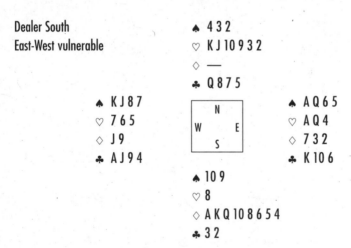

Dealer South
East-West vulnerable

♠ 4 3 2
♡ K J 10 9 3 2
◇ —
♣ Q 8 7 5

♠ K J 8 7
♡ 7 6 5
◇ J 9
♣ A J 9 4

♠ A Q 6 5
♡ A Q 4
◇ 7 3 2
♣ K 10 6

♠ 10 9
♡ 8
◇ A K Q 10 8 6 5 4
♣ 3 2

In first seat I opened a bold five diamonds. After two passes East doubled. West thought about leaving the double in, but settled for five spades. As you can see his decision was correct.

"The problem here," said Coldbottom, "is one of transverse visualization. You gave the opponents a hand to visualize and they managed it with reasonable accuracy. It was, in fact, the hand they expected you to have, and thus they were able to cope.

"I began with a bid of one notrump. My partner tried four hearts. East was in a pickle. The hand I had given him to visualize left no room in his partner's hand for any values. Being a card pusher, he could not even be sure of setting us. He remembered the sage advice of his mentors:

'Remember, my boy, you set hands with tricks; tricks, my boy, not points.' Indeed, a double might point the way for an astute declarer to bring home the contract. So discreetly he passed, and discreetly we went down four, undoubled and unvulnerable."

It was time for the final session. I thanked the Professor for his advice, and as he trundled off, as usual, to the Consolation event, I prepared to apply my new techniques in the deals to come. This one came first.

Dealer North
Both sides vulnerable

```
                      ♠ A 8 4
                      ♡ A 8 3
                      ◇ Q 7 6 3
                      ♣ K 3 2
        ♠ J 9 7                        ♠ Q 10 6 2
        ♡ J 6 5 4           N          ♡ 10 9 2
        ◇ K 10 5       W         E     ◇ A J 9 2
        ♣ Q J 10           S          ♣ 9 8
                      ♠ K 5 3
                      ♡ K Q 7
                      ◇ 8 4
                      ♣ A 7 6 5 4
```

WEST	NORTH	EAST	SOUTH
	1◇	pass	2NT
pass	3NT	all pass	

West led the queen of clubs. In the old days I would have won this with the king and led another club from dummy passing it around to West. If I was lucky, he would fail to find the killing diamond shift and often I was indeed lucky. This time I applied the rule of diminishing greed. On the queen of clubs I played small from dummy, and when East played the eight, I dropped the six from my hand. Having made the original lead with some misgivings ("Always lead a heart against notrump"), West was now convinced he had struck gold. Immediately he continued with the jack of clubs, and I ran an easy nine tricks. Chalk up one for Professor Coldbottom.

Then came this beauty. I was still South, and this was the West hand:

♠ J 5 4 ♡ K J 9 3 ◇ A K 4 ♣ A Q 2

The bidding:

WEST	NORTH	EAST	SOUTH
1NT	pass	2♣	2♡
dbl	pass	3♣	pass
3NT	pass	pass	dbl
?			

What should West do? Partner's three clubs was nonforcing, but West's hand could not be more suitable for three notrump. Maximum clubs, maximum hearts, and maximum points. Only a mouse would run! West, in fact, redoubled (to stop partner from running), and a heart was led by North. This was the layout:

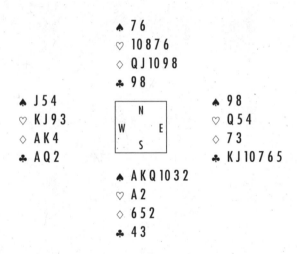

```
                    ♠ 7 6
                    ♡ 10 8 7 6
                    ◇ Q J 10 9 8
                    ♣ 9 8
   ♠ J 5 4                          ♠ 9 8
   ♡ K J 9 3          N             ♡ Q 5 4
   ◇ A K 4        W       E         ◇ 7 3
   ♣ A Q 2            S             ♣ K J 10 7 6 5
                    ♠ A K Q 10 3 2
                    ♡ A 2
                    ◇ 6 5 2
                    ♣ 4 3
```

Three down doubled and redoubled. Advanced canapé had struck again. Finally this hand came up:

♠ 2 ♡ 3 2 ◇ A K Q 8 7 6 5 4 ♣ 8 6

I began with one notrump, partner bid two clubs (Stayman), and East doubled. It now went two diamonds from me, three notrump from partner, and again double from East.

Should I sit or should I run? Partner should hold 10 to 12 high card points and a sure stopper in clubs (he too had heard the double of clubs).

One or more tricks from him plus eight from me added up to a redouble, which I duly made and everyone passed.

My assessment of partner's hand was uncannily accurate. He did in fact have a club stopper and exactly 10 points. This was his hand.

♠ K 10 5 4 ♡ K 9 8 7 ◊ — ♣ A 10 7 5 4

Partner's nice intermediate cards, plus my deceptive bidding, plus some shoddy defense, held our losses to five down.

Unfortunately, this hand cost us any chance of winning and led to some angry words from my irate partner, who failed to see that our loss had been caused not by my bidding but by an unfortunate duplication of values. I took the hand to Professor Coldbottom for adjudication.

"Here is a hand from the finals," I said. "What do you open with it?"

He gave it the merest glance. "Four diamonds," said Cornelius Coldbottom.

"But," I objected, "it's almost exactly the same hand you told me to open with one notrump this afternoon."

"It may look the same," said Coldbottom, "but it doesn't sound the same."

"But I don't hear a thing," I spluttered.

"Ah!," said the professor, "that's why you're a card pusher."

CORNELIUS COLDBOTTOM ON COMING FROM BEHIND

> *There are many high-level championship events that consist of a round-robin followed by knockout playoffs for the top few teams. Very often, the name of the game is extracting the maximum out of the weaker teams to make sure of qualifying for the next stage. As you might imagine, the Professor has some very definite views on how to go about hunting rabbits.*

"The situation is grim. It is not hopeless."

There was no mistaking the ring of conviction underlying the dry tones of Cornelius Coldbottom, premier theorist of the Wentworth Bridge and Social Club.

"One win and three losses at half-time is not an impressive Swiss Team score," he continued, "especially in an important event like the Cayuga Summer Sectional, which is apt to attract the finest of contestants. Nevertheless, I have here a chart" (he produced two sheets of paper covered with calculations) "showing that, provided certain events occur, we could still end up in a fifteen-way tie for first place.

"One thing is definite. We cannot afford another loss." He paused for a moment. "Which brings me to the point of this meeting. From here on in, because of our record, we will be playing only against pooch teams, and pooch teams are composed mainly of pooches. I haven't the time for a complete rundown on the subject. That would take a week. I can, however, cover the salient points.

"The first thing to remember is to jam the auction. Preempt every time you get the chance. The pooch has come to play. Because he hates defending, he is a bad defender; because he is a bad defender, he hates defending. Therefore, pick your level of safety using the Culbertson rule of two and three and start three levels higher. If a pooch is coming in, he will come in regardless. This is known as the Coldbottom rule of five and six.

"Secondly. Never try to lead the pooch astray in his play of the hand. Remember, the line he normally chooses is invariably the worst one. If you change his mind you are only improving his chances. Therefore, avoid your normal tools of deception. They are meaningless to him and can fool only your partner.

"My final bit of advice is this. Be a thinking man's player. The pooch never thinks. Do not be misled by his deep gaze into space, his lengthy pondering of the heavens, the eternity he takes to make a play. He is not thinking, he is posing. Emphasize that which you have and he lacks. Your bridge brains." He looked me squarely in the eye. "To fail because of lack of intelligence is a misfortune. To fail because of lack of thought is a crime."

These were the professor's final words. The directorial bellow summoned us back to the field of combat, and we sat down for the second half of the tournament.

The very first deal produced an example of the Coldbottom teachings. The professor and I were seated East and West. We were vulnerable and the opponents were not, and this was the South hand:

♠ 1074 ♡ A2 ◇ AKQ1096 ♣ 42

North was the dealer and passed. Coldbottom also passed, and South opened one diamond. I overcalled two spades (intermediate, showing a good suit and an opening bid), and North bid three diamonds. Professor Coldbottom raised the ante to four spades, and it was squarely up to South. What should he do? Tactics, the favorable vulnerability, the principle of insurance, all cried out for a bid of five diamonds. After much squirming he finally made the call. I doubled and everyone passed. I led the king of spades, and this was the layout:

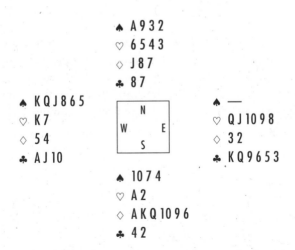

The contract was not a comfortable one. The ace of spades was put up for decapitation, and we still had to come to two more spades, two clubs and a heart. Down four doubled. As you can see, four spades would not have been a success.

The imaginative raise on a void brought us a win. We were also victorious in the second match, ending up a lopsided 7 IMPs ahead, as our partners bid and made three slams not reached at our table. The third match was a ding-dong affair, and our cause was not helped when Coldbottom presented me with a defensive headache.

$$\spadesuit \ J\,8\,7\,2$$
$$\heartsuit \ A\,Q\,10\,6\,3$$
$$\diamond \ K\,J$$
$$\clubsuit \ 9\,4$$

Me

$$\spadesuit \ A\,9\,6$$
$$\heartsuit \ K\,J\,9\,7\,4$$
$$\diamond \ 4\,3$$
$$\clubsuit \ A\,6\,5$$

	N	
W		E
	S	

WEST	NORTH	EAST	SOUTH
Me		Coldbottom	
1♡	pass	1♠	2◇
pass	2♡	pass	3◇
pass	5◇	dbl	all pass

I led the ace of spades, getting the seven from dummy, the king from Coldbottom, and a small one from declarer. My partner's dramatic card could only be calling for an equally dramatic shift. "What can it be but a heart?" thought I, as I duly led the four of that suit. It went ten from dummy, deuce from partner — and a small club from declarer! These were the four hands:

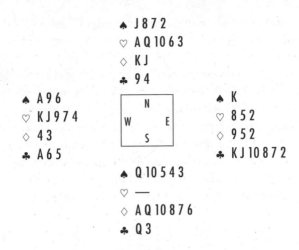

```
                    ♠ J 8 7 2
                    ♡ A Q 10 6 3
                    ◇ K J
                    ♣ 9 4
    ♠ A 9 6          ┌─────────┐      ♠ K
    ♡ K J 9 7 4      │    N    │      ♡ 8 5 2
    ◇ 4 3            │ W     E │      ◇ 9 5 2
    ♣ A 6 5          │    S    │      ♣ K J 10 8 7 2
                     └─────────┘
                    ♠ Q 10 5 4 3
                    ♡ —
                    ◇ A Q 10 8 7 6
                    ♣ Q 3
```

Declarer threw his second club on the ace of hearts, pulled trumps and made six. At the other table our teammates, playing in four spades, went down one as the defense collected two clubs and two spades.

As usual, my argument with partner proved unrewarding. I reminded him of his warning against psyching. He advised me that his rules were made for lesser mortals. I repeated his remarks about a "thinking" player. He told me to keep my mind uncluttered. "A high card means continue the suit," he said, "a low one means switch."

Luckily our partners had another sparkling session, and we squeaked through a winner to the final round. Who should our opponents prove to be but our hated rivals, the famous "Blue Team" from the village of Stoney Creek. If we lost to them, we would hear about it for months.

The professor chose to oppose what he considered to be the strong half of their team, Darryl Sly and Willie "the Weeper" Schplatz. The cards were very tight, and as we reached the last board I had the uneasy feeling that an IMP one way or the other might swing the match. What a time to look upon the following:

♠ K J 10 9 8 7 6 ♡ 5 ◇ J 10 6 ♣ 3 2

"Jam the auction," Coldbottom had said. Well, jam it I would. But how high? The rule of Culbertson called for a three-bid, the rule of Coldbottom called for the six-level. I decided to compromise.

"I am about to skip the bidding," I said. "Five spades."

Darryl Sly waited his customary one-tenth of a second and passed, my partner passed, and Schplatz bid a firm five notrump, which became the final contract.

What should a thinking man do? To be passive and lead a diamond or to attack with a spade, that was the question. Clearly Schplatz was taking a shot. No doubt he had one spade stopper and a long suit. If that was the case, then the answer was easy. A hero leads a spade, a pipsqueak leads a diamond.

Once I decided on a spade, it wasn't even close as to which one was the expert choice — the king, of course, in the hope of crashing a singleton honor in dummy. I produced it with a flourish. It was a triumph for reasoning, as a singleton honor did indeed appear in dummy.

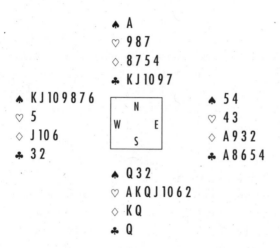

```
              ♠ A
              ♡ 987
              ◇ 8754
              ♣ KJ1097
♠ KJ1098 76   ┌───────┐   ♠ 54
♡ 5           │   N   │   ♡ 43
◇ J106        │ W   E │   ◇ A932
♣ 32          │   S   │   ♣ A8654
              └───────┘
              ♠ Q32
              ♡ AKQJ10 62
              ◇ KQ
              ♣ Q
```

By "smothering" the ace of spades, I gave Schplatz a second spade stopper and time to knock out the ace of clubs. The lead of a small spade sets him three tricks; the lead of the jack of diamonds, two. It was the right girl but the wrong time and place.

The ride home took place in dismal quiet. We knew in our hearts that our loss to the Blue Team was going to produce a lot of nasty questions back at the club. Finally, one of our teammates interrupted the silence.

"How come they made five notrump on Board 15?" he asked. It was left to Professor Coldbottom to reply.

"Some declarers are born great," he said, "some achieve greatness, and some manage to get my partner on lead."

"The right wording," I said stiffly, "is 'some have greatness thrust upon them.'"

"It comes," said Cornelius Coldbottom, "to exactly the same thing."

THE CURSE OF THE BLUE TEAM

There is no doubt that the Italian Blue Team contained some great players: Belladonna, Garozzo and Forquet are generally acknowledged to have been among the best of all time. But not their teammates, which in itself raises questions about the phenomenal success of the squad. Bobby Wolff, in The Lone Wolff, *characterized most of the other all-conquering Italians as "average club players". So while this story is placed in a humorous setting, I may not be alone in feeling that Frank had a more serious message in mind. Alan Sontag once said to me, "You always know when you're being cheated. You may not know exactly what they are doing, but you know something is going on." Alan Truscott, in* The Great Bridge Scandal, *pointed out how hard it is to prove cheating from hand records. But think about it at the end of this piece and see whether you too don't come to the conclusion that, just maybe, something was going on.*

When they write the definitive history of bridge in the twentieth century, surely one of its most glowing chapters will relate the phenomenal story of that superb Canadian Quartet, the heralded Blue Team from Stoney Creek. For twelve years without fail they have brought home that granddaddy of all bridge prizes, the Chicken Roost Trophy, emblem of bridge supremacy in Southern Ontario.

Several explanations have been advanced for this unbroken string of victories. Some credit their unique bidding philosophy. As you doubtless know, they play the very stylized Buller system, named after Colonel Walter Buller of England, whose guiding principle is no artificial conventions. None! As you can imagine, it is very frustrating to play against someone who calls a spade a spade. (For instance, an opponent opens the bidding one club, natural... is your bidding system designed to cope with this?) Others point to their fine team spirit and discipline. (No wives at training camp; one temper tantrum per board limit; and so on.) Finally there is the sour grapes brigade.

"It's nothing but luck. Plain dumb luck. That's their secret, pure and simple." This bellow came from George Loudmouth, one of the charter members of The Wentworth Bridge and Social Club and a man known for his loud convictions. "Listen to me," he advised, "I've played against them for years. Whenever they're right they're right, and even when they're wrong they're right."

"Dear fellow. You are mistaken, totally mistaken. What you call luck is simply flair." This time the speaker was Professor Cornelius Coldbottom, president emeritus of the club and the finest bidder in the world. "Study the great matches of history," he continued, "and you will see that at each critical juncture the master player will take a winning action that would never occur to any of us. Learn to emulate their methods and then perhaps our day will also come."

As between Loudmouth's fatalistic philosophy (after all what can you do about luck?) and Coldbottom's optimistic advice, it was easy for me to opt for the latter, and for three solid months preceding the championship event I studied and memorized each hand from every Bermuda Bowl and Olympiad contest of the past fifteen years. I was a walking encyclopedia of bridge.

And nothing happened! We had finished all but three boards of the contest and not one single solitary thing had come up. Perhaps George was right. They were just too lucky. I was playing in partnership with Loudmouth and we were facing the strong half of the Blue Team, the seasoned pair of Eric Murphy and Sammy Cartwheels. My estimate of the match to this point was that it was excruciatingly close and that everything would probably hinge on the results of these last few boards. It was then I picked up this hand:

♠ 85 ♡ 9 ◇ A 10 7 6 3 ♣ A 9 8 6

You recognize the hand, of course. It is from Board 76 of the 1968 Olympiad finals between Italy and the USA, and it was held by Camillo Pabis-Ticci. The bidding against him proceeded one spade by Arthur Robinson, two hearts by Robert Jordan, two spades by Robinson, three spades by Jordan, four spades by Robinson; and Pabis-Ticci found himself on lead. He put down the ace of clubs!

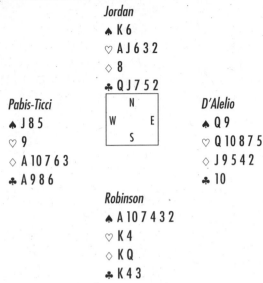

Jordan
♠ K 6
♡ A J 6 3 2
◇ 8
♣ Q J 7 5 2

Pabis-Ticci
♠ J 8 5
♡ 9
◇ A 10 7 6 3
♣ A 9 8 6

D'Alelio
♠ Q 9
♡ Q 10 8 7 5
◇ J 9 5 4 2
♣ 10

Robinson
♠ A 10 7 4 3 2
♡ K 4
◇ K Q
♣ K 4 3

As you can see, the lead was a spectacular one. D'Alelio ruffed the club continuation, led back to his partner's ace of diamonds, and got himself another club ruff to set the contract. At the other table the contract was unbeatable after the pedestrian lead of the singleton heart. It could not have come at a better time for the Italians. The Americans, far behind all through the match, had rallied to within 11 IMPs of the leaders. As *Bridge World* reporter Tony Trad put it, "Avarelli and Belladonna, who were sitting out, were pacing nervously up and down in the Bridgerama room, fearing the end of Italy's streak." This hand, however, was the *coup de grâce*. More interesting than the lead was Pabis-Ticci's explanation for it. He stated that he had seen Robinson lead the ace of clubs against a partscore on Bridgerama the day before and that had proved to be the only way to defeat the contract. He thought it would be nice if Robinson were "hoist with his own petard".

The bidding against us went exactly the same way and once again the contract was four spades. With a flourish I produced the lead of the ace of clubs. This time, however, the cards were distributed just a little differently.

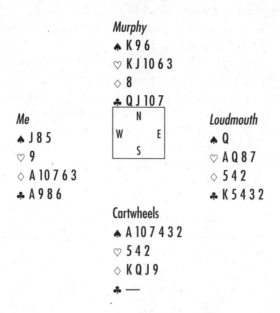

Murphy
♠ K 9 6
♡ K J 10 6 3
◇ 8
♣ Q J 10 7

Me
♠ J 8 5
♡ 9
◇ A 10 7 6 3
♣ A 9 8 6

Loudmouth
♠ Q
♡ A Q 8 7
◇ 5 4 2
♣ K 5 4 3 2

Cartwheels
♠ A 10 7 4 3 2
♡ 5 4 2
◇ K Q J 9
♣ —

Declarer trumped my ace of clubs, laid down the ace of spades, reached dummy by finessing against my jack of trumps and led the queen of clubs, ruffing out Loudmouth's king. He returned to dummy with the king of spades and discarded two losers on the good clubs. Four spades bid and made. My partner was visibly upset. "What kind of idiot lead is that?" he screamed. "Any normal human being, if he wants a ruff, leads his short suit, or his long suit if he wants to give partner a ruff. What kind of cretin leads a short suit to give a ruff? Are you out of your mind?"

"I led it," I explained, "because I once saw Arthur Robinson lead the ace of clubs against a partscore on Bridgerama, and that was the only way to set the contract."

For some reason this failed to soothe my partner, who began to froth at the mouth. Even the opponents got into the act, and I thought I heard someone say something about "ask a foolish question and you get a foolish answer". I have to admit that when you say it out loud the reasoning for the lead seems to lose a lot of its persuasiveness.

Now there were only two boards left, and you can imagine my emotions as I looked at my next hand:

♠ 6 ♡ 8 7 6 3 ◇ 9 6 ♣ A K 8 7 5 2

It is, of course, from Deal 77 from the 1967 Bermuda Bowl, and these were the cards held by the holy one himself, Pietro Forquet. He heard the bidding go: one spade on his left, double from his partner, four spades on his right, everybody vulnerable.

Instead of the expected five hearts or five clubs, Forquet surprised the world by doubling. The contract was defeated one trick after the ace-king and another diamond, which Forquet ruffed. Later, Garozzo won a heart trick. Since the responder was void of clubs, neither five clubs nor five hearts could be made. As Monroe Ingberman, reporting for *The Bridge World*, put it, "Forquet's judgment on such hands is remarkable, and he has won many points for the Blue Team in this fashion."

Sure enough, the bidding went one spade on my left, double from my partner and four spades on my right. Naturally, I doubled. George led the ace-king and another diamond and we did even better than the Italians, in that the contract was down two, no one being void in clubs. This was partner's hand:

♠ — ♡ K Q J 4 ◇ A K 8 3 2 ♣ Q 9 4 3

Because of the lucky lie of the cards, we were also cold for slam in either of two suits. Loudmouth, who has a great tendency to result hands, could not stop commenting on this fact. I couldn't seem to convince him that six was there only because of the freakish distribution of the opponents' cards, i.e., no void in clubs, no singleton heart. When I brought up the name of Forquet he muttered darkly something about there being more than one kind of nut in the forest.

As you may suspect, I was a little downhearted as we came to the last deal of the contest. It seemed that, barring a miracle, the match was hopelessly out the window. What a time to pick up the following collection.

♠ 7 6 4 3 2 ♡ J 10 9 4 ◇ K Q 4 ♣ 2

It was, of course, the famous "cool" hand of the 1957 World Championship, which many observers have claimed was decisive in shattering American morale. Let me quote from the writings of Alphonse Moyse Jr. in his report of the event.

"With both sides vulnerable, West dealt and bid one club, and this was the North holding:

♠ 7 6 4 3 2 ♡ J 10 9 4 ◇ K Q 4 ♣ 2

'One spade,' said Siniscalco coolly.

"I heard the bid, I saw the hand — and a few minutes later I wanted to call off the few bets I had made on the match. South turned up with:

♠ A 5 ♡ A 8 6 5 2 ◇ 10 9 2 ♣ K Q 5

"South, Forquet, bid two notrump. Siniscalco bid three hearts (just as coolly), and Forquet bid four hearts. The adverse trumps were 2-2 and the intrepid Italians paid out a measly 100 points for their fun.

"Speaking very quietly and confidentially to myself, I said, 'This is bad. Anyone who doesn't go down at least 800 on that spade overcall, bidding system or no system, is just too omniscient or too something for us simple Americans. The handwriting is on the wall.'"

Sure enough, my vulnerable opponent opened one club. Coolly I over-called one spade. Here the script changed, as Murphy on my left doubled. Partner, no doubt surprised by all the bidding, passed. Just as coolly I removed to two hearts and Murphy doubled again.

"Aha," I thought, "I may get it all back on this one board. Two hearts doubled plus an overtrick, let's see — that's 870. I'd better redouble and make it 1190."

Coolly I redoubled, and everyone passed. Murphy led the king of hearts and my dummy was a little disappointing:

♠ 8 5 ♡ Q 8 3 ◇ 10 9 7 3 ♣ K Q 6 4

I managed to score two trumps, a club and a diamond. I had miscalculated the number. It was not 1190, it was 2200.

As my opponents reeled off trick after trick, my partner sat there in paralyzed silence. It was not until the deal was well over that he managed to regain his voice, by this time a hoarse croak. "And who was this one in honor of," he asked, "Ely Culbertson?"

As coolly as I could (under the circumstances I was a little upset) I explained about Siniscalco and the 1957 World Championship.

"You know," said Loudmouth, "there's one thing all those guys you're telling me about have got that you haven't got."

"I know," I said despondently, "flair."

"No," said Loudmouth, "what they've got is luckier partners."

You know something, I think he's right.

COLDBOTTOM ON PRACTICAL BRIDGE

> *A fair amount of bridge literature has been generated by writers talking about how to come from behind in a team game. There are plenty of techniques available for generating swings, some recommended and some not. But I know of little if anything that talks about how to preserve a lead. The Professor is certainly right about one thing: in some ways it's harder to play from the front. The underdogs, trailing in the match, have little to lose. The overdogs will naturally find a measure of caution creeping into their game, as they seek to hang on to the gains made to date. What they forget is that abandoning the style of play that got them those gains is unlikely to be as successful…*

"Who wins at bridge? The record is clear. It is the practical player." The speaker was Professor Cornelius Coldbottom, dean of the world's great bridge authorities and president emeritus of the Wentworth Bridge and Social Club. We were between sessions of the Cayuga Bowl; our opponents, as usual, were those constant winners, the dread Blue Team from Stoney Creek. For the first time in living memory we were not hopelessly behind. The Professor, however, had come to warn us, not to praise us.

"Since we are ahead," he said, "there will be a tendency to sit on our lead, to nurture those two precious IMPs. Therein lies the road to disaster. We must instead play the dashing game, match the daring of our opponents. One word of caution, however; remember, always be a practical player. Do not emulate those dreamers who spend their time in a futile quest for the impossible dream, who go from hand to hand (was he looking at me?) pursuing one great moment of glory that will make them immortal, and plodding instead into the swamp. Let this be your motto: The play that works is the play that's right. Some might call that being a resulter. I call it being a winner."

It was time to go back to the battle, I playing in the Open Room with Harry Loudmouth. For a time, things were uneventful. Then came a chance to use a special convention. My left-hand opponent opened the bidding with one notrump. Partner passed, and my RHO raised to three notrump. I held:

♠ A K Q J 6 ♡ 4 3 ◇ 4 3 2 ♣ A 4 3

My partner and I play that a double in this position promises a solid suit and asks partner to "find the lead". Normally he picks his shortest suit, since this is apt to be my longest. So I doubled and everyone passed. Loudmouth went into convulsions and finally found the lead... a small heart! These were the four hands:

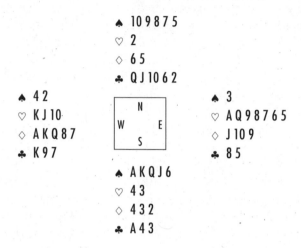

♠ 10 9 8 7 5
♡ 2
◇ 6 5
♣ Q J 10 6 2

♠ 4 2
♡ K J 10
◇ A K Q 8 7
♣ K 9 7

♠ 3
♡ A Q 9 8 7 6 5
◇ J 10 9
♣ 8 5

♠ A K Q J 6
♡ 4 3
◇ 4 3 2
♣ A 4 3

As you can see, our opponents had bid their cards like two maniacs, jeopardizing a sound four hearts for the sketchy notrump game. Nevertheless, since they had made their contract with three doubled, vulnerable overtricks, I felt it was possible we had lost IMPs on the board. Remembering the Professor's admonition, I immediately assessed the blame.

"Wrong lead, partner," I said. "You blew it again."

Loudmouth was frothing at the mouth. "The stupid convention was your stupid idea," he bellowed, "and in the second place, you're the one who told me it calls for a short-suit lead."

"If you're going to play high-level bridge," I said in lofty tones, "you will have to learn when to overrule your partner's suggestions."

One word led to another, and somehow Loudmouth decided to exchange seats with Professor Coldbottom. It was not long before we came to another hand of interest. I was still South, and picked up as dealer:

♠ A 5 ♡ K 2 ◇ A K 10 9 3 ♣ K 5 4 3

I opened the bidding classically with one notrump. Coldbottom tried for a major-suit fit with a Stayman bid, then settled for three notrump. West led the eight of spades, and this is what I saw:

♠ 4 3
♡ A 9 8 7
◇ 7 6
♣ A J 10 7 6

```
      N
  W       E
      S
```

♠ A 5
♡ K 2
◇ A K 10 9 3
♣ K 5 4 3

I won the spade and tested the clubs. They were 2-2. I could see that six clubs was a piece of cake, and no doubt we should be there. My partner had certainly shown a lack of appreciation for his excellent controls and distribution. Coldbottom, of all people, had turned into a point-counter!

If my opponents reached the slam, we were destined to lose a bushel of IMPs and there was nothing I could do about that. However, remembering Coldbottom's advice, I took time out to concentrate. What would the practical player do? Then it came to me as if in a vision. If I took my ten top tricks and scored 430 points and they bid the slam in the other room, I would lose 10 IMPs. If, however, I found a lucky lie in diamonds (doubleton queen-jack), or if my right-hand opponent held queen-jack and another and played carelessly, I might bring in all thirteen tricks for a score of 520 and gain one precious IMP. Not that I intended anything like a double finesse at Trick 1. That would be reckless. Still, it couldn't hurt to lead one little diamond, so I traveled to the dummy and played the six. Sure enough, my right-hand opponent, Benito Yardstick, planked down the queen. I won the king, went back to dummy with a club, and put through a second diamond. When Benito played small, I smoothly produced the ten-spot. There are not too many players brave enough to make that play.

This was the full deal:

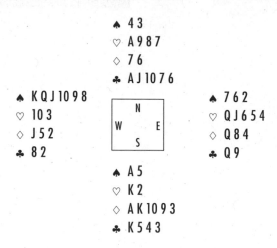

<pre>
          ♠ 4 3
          ♡ A 9 8 7
          ◇ 7 6
          ♣ A J 10 7 6
♠ K Q J 10 9 8   ♠ 7 6 2
♡ 10 3   N   ♡ Q J 6 5 4
◇ J 5 2   W   E   ◇ Q 8 4
♣ 8 2   S   ♣ Q 9
          ♠ A 5
          ♡ K 2
          ◇ A K 10 9 3
          ♣ K 5 4 3
</pre>

As you can see, it was not quite the success story of the year. Once again the percentage play had failed. I was pointing this out to Coldbottom, when I noticed his face had turned a mottled purple color. Really the strain of these high-level games was getting too much for the Professor. I decided to table the discussion for later.

As often happens, the cards turned flattish, and nothing of interest came up until the very last board. It was a classic "how do you play the suit?" situation.

♠ A K J 9 4

♠ 8 6 3

The problem is to lose no tricks in the suit. In my younger simplistic days, I always finessed for the queen. Not being very learned, I thought it was the correct play; and to tell the truth, more often than not it worked. Then along came Edgar Kaplan, and in an article entitled "The Deep Nine" he proved that in most cases it was right to finesse the nine. His was a compli- cated theory based on the cards played to the first trick and the ages of the players. What you do, he claimed, is first lay down the ace. If the player sitting over dummy plays a card other than the queen or ten, you come back to your hand and lead up again. If a small card appears on your left, then:

(a) If your right-hand opponent is more than sixty years of age or less than twenty, you finesse the nine, since players in these age brackets tend to falsecard all the time and would have produced the ten the first time the suit was played had they had it, and so they don't have it which means the other one has it, or else you've had it, or something like that. (I think that's it, Edgar.)

(b) If your RHO is over twenty and less than sixty, it is best to finesse the jack unless you are playing computer hands, in which case you always play to drop the doubleton queen offside.

Clearly it was important to know the age of my opponent. "How old is your partner?" I asked West, Omar Bellaroma.

"He has just celebrated his sixty-third birthday," Omar replied.

It just goes to show that you can never tell with these Latin types. I would never have put him past his thirties. Naturally I led the six of spades, and when West played the five I finessed the nine... losing to East's doubleton ten.

"By the way," said Benito, "my partner was a little confused about my birthday. It was not my sixty-third I just celebrated, it was my thirty-sixth." Well, once again the Blue Team from Stoney Creek are the champions of Southern Ontario. At least this time they know they were in a fight, as we succumbed by an unnerving 3 IMPs. As you can imagine, our team had many boards where we could have picked up this small deficit, although (and I say it modestly) in retrospect I cannot see any hand that I should have played differently. At least I was glad to see the Edgar Kaplan theory proven right. I couldn't have stood it if he had been wrong. He's my hero, you know. I try to model my bridge after his. That's why I'm sending this story to *The Bridge World*. So he can know what he's accomplished.

HE WHO HOLDS THE LONG SUIT

Fred Gitelman expressed the theme of this piece very well in a "How to Improve Your Game" article in Canadian Master Point *magazine back in the 1990s, stating simply: Don't play to get into the* Daily Bulletin. *Wall Street investors know this as well; the saying there is that bulls make money and bears make money, but pigs lose.*

"Open any book on bridge and what do you find? Pages devoted to bidding, play and opening leads, the trivia of bridge... but precious little on the subject of tactics."

The speaker was Professor Cornelius Coldbottom, the thinking man's player. "It is a pity, really," he continued, "since a proper application of tactics is worth a fortune in matchpoints. Yet, its frequency of use is distinguished only by infrequency. All this in respect to a teachable discipline founded on those two great principles: the doctrine of elegance, and the theory of beclouding of vision." He paused to clear his throat. "I will elucidate.

"There is a growing body of players to whom bridge is no longer a game of win or lose. It has become, instead, a pursuit of glory where everyone wants to be a star. Let me give you an example.

"South is in seven notrump after an uncontested auction, with:

♠ A 2
♡ A Q 6 3 2
◇ K Q
♣ Q J 9 7

```
       N
   W       E
       S
```

♠ 6 3
♡ 5 4
◇ A J 10 9 8 7
♣ A K 3

"To a sensible player, the issue is simple. Either the heart finesse works or he is going down. Stars look more deeply into the cards. They see that if East holds an eight-card spade suit and the king of hearts he can be squeezed. Remote? Absurd? Of course! But you do not get your name in the papers by taking a simple finesse, and you will find a whole army of players gallantly trying to drop the singleton king of hearts offside.

"Where does tactics fit into all this? Tactics is to bid or play your cards in such a way that your opponent gets his chance to be a star. And stars, as we all know, have this irresistible compulsion to end up in the soup.

"The same holds true for beclouding of vision. When partner opens one diamond and you hold six hearts to the ace-queen-jack and a few other high cards, the only question is how many hearts to bid. But when the opponent overcalls one heart ahead of you, you have many options. Double, pass, some number of notrump, some number of hearts — all these would get votes in the Master Solvers' Club. If your opponent has made his bid holding no hearts, he has achieved, for good or evil, a triumph of tactics. You may land on your feet or fall on your head, but you have beyond question had your vision beclouded."

As usual, the Professor had given me much to think about. I returned to the battle, eager to apply my new knowledge.

The first few rounds of the Consolation were tame, and we had been getting mediocre results when an exciting deal showed up. East-West were vulnerable and we were not, and West began proceedings with two notrump. Coldbottom overcalled three clubs and East bid three notrump. I was South, and this was my hand:

♠ Q J 8 3 2 ♡ — ◇ 9 4 2 ♣ J 9 6 5 4

I could double or pass and hope a club lead would set it. That did not seem likely. I could bid four or five clubs as a sacrifice against vulnerable opponents. That seemed more reasonable. I decided instead to becloud their vision.

"Four hearts," I said. It was the perfect call. Someone might double, then I would scurry back to clubs; and if somehow they settled in a suit contract, a heart lead from partner would be very nice indeed.

West duly doubled, Coldbottom passed, as did East, and I converted to five clubs as planned. Once again West doubled and this time Coldbottom bid the hearts, five of them. East doubled. I gritted my teeth. The professor was certainly being obtuse. Nevertheless, it was my job to end up in the best partnership spot, not to bemoan partner's lack of insight. Since there was no point starting out a bidding war with my own partner, I made the one call that would force him to return to clubs. I redoubled. Partner had heard me run from the double of four hearts. Clearly this could not be to play. Alas, all passed with varying degrees of relish.

These were the four hands:

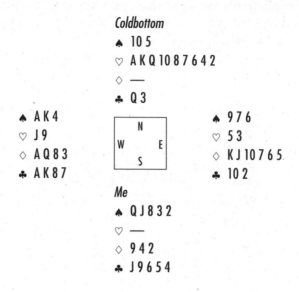

Coldbottom
♠ 10 5
♡ A K Q 10 8 7 6 4 2
♢ —
♣ Q 3

♠ A K 4
♡ J 9
♢ A Q 8 3
♣ A K 8 7

♠ 9 7 6
♡ 5 3
♢ K J 10 7 6 5
♣ 10 2

Me
♠ Q J 8 3 2
♡ —
♢ 9 4 2
♣ J 9 6 5 4

Minus 600 was not too far removed from par. The opponents can make five diamonds on a club-spade squeeze. I pointed this out to Coldbottom, but for once he seemed to have lost his fabled objectivity.

"The best tactics for you," he said, "is to pass at every legal opportunity."

A short time later came a second chance. This time I held the long suit:

♠ A K Q J 5 3 2 ♡ 6 5 ♢ 5 4 2 ♣ 2

The young girl on my right opened one diamond. They were vulnerable and we were not. I knew what would happen around the room. A large, unimaginative group would bid four spades. A smaller, more cunning faction would overcall one spade and be hauled upstairs kicking and screaming. I chose to pass. I would let my opponents get in a round or two of bidding, and then I would overcall in spades at the appropriate level. They would be completely befuddled.

It worked like a charm. I passed and the elderly gentleman on my left bid one heart. Unfortunately, East decided that the appropriate level was four notrump. Gallantly I jammed the auction with a bid of six spades. This went down four, doubled, a very nice save against their cold vulnerable slam. Again Coldbottom was not pleased. He felt that an immediate spade bid would end any chance of the opponents' finding the heart fit. I could not see the logic of his argument. Surely most players would find a negative double over a four-spade bid. Just look at the two hands:

```
     ♠ 7 6 4                         ♠ 10
     ♡ K 4 3 2          N            ♡ A Q 8 7
     ◇ Q 3           W     E         ◇ A K 9 8 7 6
     ♣ J 8 3 2          S            ♣ A 4
```

Nevertheless, I could see that my concentration on tactics was leading to dissension in the ranks, so I decided to abandon this phase of activity for the time being and concentrate on plain bridge. In this context, one very interesting situation came up. This was the bidding with the opponents vulnerable and no interference from us (I have turned the directions to make the declarer South):

NORTH	SOUTH
1◇	2♠
3◇	4♣
4♠	6♠
pass	

Coldbottom led the seven of hearts, and this was the dummy I saw:

```
              Dummy
              ♠ A 3
              ♡ J 5 4
              ◇ A Q 8 7 5
              ♣ Q 6 4
                              Me
                              ♠ 6 5 4
              N               ♡ 10 6 3
          W       E           ◇ 4 3 2
              S               ♣ 7 5 3 2
```

The declarer played low from dummy, I inserted the ten — and it held! My partner had underled a suit of six to the ace-king-queen! Why? The obvious answer was that he wanted a ruff, and the only ruffable suit appeared to be diamonds. Hold on a moment, though. What was it that Coldbottom always used to say? "The highest aspiration of the palooka is to perceive the obvious." And so I began to think.

For the professor to be void in diamonds, the declarer would have had to suppress five-card support. Unlikely. Moreover, the underlead of a suit for ruffing purposes was your standard bread-and-butter type of brilliant play, not really typical of Coldbottom's methods. Then, in a burst of brilliance, it came to me. He didn't want a ruff. He wanted me to break up a squeeze. The entire deal seemed to pass in front of my eyes like a vision. If there was any justice in the world, this just had to be the layout:

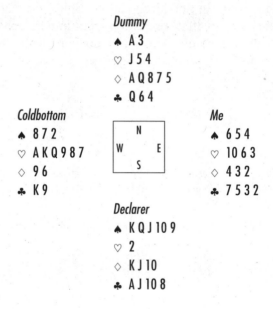

Dummy
♠ A 3
♡ J 5 4
♢ A Q 8 7 5
♣ Q 6 4

Coldbottom
♠ 8 7 2
♡ A K Q 9 8 7
♢ 9 6
♣ K 9

Me
♠ 6 5 4
♡ 10 6 3
♢ 4 3 2
♣ 7 5 3 2

Declarer
♠ K Q J 10 9
♡ 2
♢ K J 10
♣ A J 10 8

If West leads a heart and then a second heart, declarer runs all the trumps and the diamonds, coming down to this position with the lead in dummy:

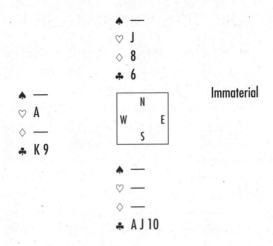

♠ —
♡ J
♢ 8
♣ 6

♠ —
♡ A
♢ —
♣ K 9

```
    N
 W     E
    S
```

Immaterial

♠ —
♡ —
♢ —
♣ A J 10

On the lead of the last diamond declarer discards his ten of clubs. West is skewered. If he keeps two clubs, the jack of hearts in dummy is high; and if he keeps the high heart then his club king will fall under the ace. By returning a club, however, I break up the squeeze. Coldbottom's great underlead and my equally laudable perception meant that we were about to participate in a deal for the ages. As I returned the five of clubs, I could already see my name in the papers.

A grateful declarer scooped up my club lead with the king and ran his twelve top tricks. This was his hand:

♠ K Q J 10 9   ♡ 2   ♢ K J 10 9 6   ♣ A K

The lead was perfect. The return was perfect. Only the cards were wrong. I swallowed painfully, repressing a rueful smile.

"It certainly proves your theory of elegance," I said. "Imagine any sane person suppressing five-card support for his partner's suit just to play in an inferior slam."

"I can," said Coldbottom, "think of an even better example from the same deal."

Now, I wonder what he meant by that.

COLDBOTTOM ON SPORTSMANSHIP

> Discretion in enforcing the laws of the game is still a controversial topic. Only this year, a well-known US expert playing in a top competition was heavily criticized for allowing his opponent to retract a cardplay error that the expert believed to have been caused by his own overlong tank. I was playing a Swiss Teams a year or so ago when the auction began 2♠ (weak) from my partner, double, pass; at this point LHO deposited a green card on the table, not having seen her partner's double. It never occurred to me to do anything but allow her to change her bid. But what surprised me was how effusively grateful she was; throughout the day she would draw people's attention to the incident, citing it as an example of extreme sportsmanship. I just think it's the way the game should be played, and I know Frank Vine felt the same way. But then, I've never played the final of a Bermuda Bowl, so perhaps I would feel differently in that situation.

"Carrot! Termite! Renegade!" The abuse came from Professor Cornelius Coldbottom, sage emeritus of the Wentworth Bridge and Social Club. I had never seen him so angry. The target of the barrage was Harry Loudmouth, one of our senior players. The occasion was the Cayuga Mixed Pairs.

A group of us under the leadership of Coldbottom had decided that the time was ripe for Canada to make a direct challenge for the Bermuda Bowl. We knew it was vital to practice against tough opponents. To that end, we had arranged to attend our first National tournament shortly, in a far off American city. Meanwhile, we were playing in fixed partnerships in all local events.

The deal had come up during the evening session. Loudmouth was the dealer, and on his left sat Elias Culvert, 96 years of age, somewhat frail and dim of vision but still a feared competitor. Loudmouth had rocked back in his chair as he was sorting his cards, jostling the arm of a passing caddy, who proceeded to dump a jug of ice water all over Culvert, short-circuiting his hearing aid and causing him to drop all his cards. Confused by all this, Culvert opened the bidding out of turn, one spade. We all knew the penalty for this heinous crime. If Loudmouth passed, the bidding would continue normally; if he bid, though, Culvert's partner was barred for the rest* of the auction. Looking at a balanced yarborough, Loudmouth passed, whereupon Culvert reached a hopeless slam, which made, however, when there was an accident on lead.

As Loudmouth put it, "I wiped him off, I picked him up, and I led out of turn. What else did you want me to do?"

Coldbottom replied that what he wanted him to do was to open the bidding: one spade for choice, so that partner would know he had psyched. When the rest of us expressed astonishment at this point of view, Coldbottom withered us with his scorn. "Where have you been these last few years? Haven't you heard about the new sportsmanship? Read *The Bridge World* and learn." He directed us to the landmark issue of April, 1977, and to all subsequent expositions by the editorial staff and their supporters, on the fine art of being a good sport.

It wasn't easy. Some of us found ourselves barred from the rubber bridge tables. No one would let us cut in. It was a relief to learn from Coldbottom that his rules did not apply to rubber bridge. "Those hayseeds are only playing for money," he explained. "They can afford to be friendly. We are dealing in masterpoints and cannot indulge in frivolities."

Others were having trouble distinguishing between fighting fierce and fighting foul. Here was a problem faced by Harry Loudmouth, South.

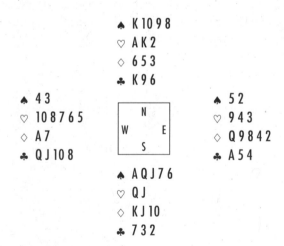

His contract was four spades, and the lady on his left thumped down the ace of diamonds, hoping for a quick ruff. When her partner played the

---

* Maybe you should have called the director — if Culvert bids spades at his proper turn, partner is barred only for *this* round of bidding. —Edgar Kaplan

deuce, a club shift seemed inevitable — until Loudmouth changed her mind.

"Pardon me," he inquired. "Do you lead the ace from ace-king?"

"No," the lady muttered as she shot out a second diamond.

"That's nice," said Harry as he shoveled in the trick and proceeded to ice his contract.

The committee was hostile, but Harry stuck to his guns. He insisted that his question was motivated solely by his interest in the carding agreements of his opponents (for future reference, he said). He didn't neglect to point out the questionable ethics of his left-hand opponent who had fired out the second diamond like a torpedo in the face of partner's discouraging two-spot. "If they were playing upside-down signals," Harry said, "shouldn't they Alert us?"

Coldbottom spent two hours that night spelling out the difference between sportsmanship and gamesmanship. To most of us it seemed hard to distinguish.

And so we arrived at the Nationals. What a thrill to meet the storied giants of the game, whom none of us had ever seen! I made sure to point out those I recognized to Coldbottom to insure he would be suitably apprehensive.

Our first important encounter came on the third round. Our opponents were certainly somebodies, for the table was engulfed by kibitzers. One smoked a meerschaum and the other was called Norman. It was all affability until the second board.

Dealer South
East-West vulnerable

Norman
♠ A K 6 5 4
♡ 6
◇ A K
♣ A K Q J 10

Me
♠ 9 3 2
♡ J 10 8 7
◇ 7 5 4 3
♣ 4 3

```
       N
   W       E
       S
```

Coldbottom
♠ Q
♡ Q 9 5 2
◇ 9 8 6 2
♣ 7 6 5 2

Pipesmoker
♠ J 10 8 7
♡ A K 4 3
◇ Q J 10
♣ 9 8

The bidding was unexceptional. South opened a weak notrump and North put him in seven. I led the jack of hearts. The declarer let this come to his hand, puffed three times on his pipe, and pushed out the jack of spades. Whoa, I said to myself, I've got a problem.

I could play the deuce and give count. I could ignore count and play a deceptive three, or I could pop the nine and try to muddle the communications. I took out one card, put it back, pulled out another, put it back, and so on for about four minutes. Finally I played the three. The pipesmoker studied this, studied me, and finally finessed.

The director was polite but inquisitive. Why had I hesitated? I advised him that it was not hesitation, it was thought. Thinking and huddling, I explained, though very different, often appear similar to an opponent. Luckily I was able to cite chapter and verse, namely the June *Bridge World*, page 26, where an identical situation had been carefully reviewed. I quoted the author. "If we had been hesitating over which card to play (whether to falsecard, whether to give count), we would say nothing. If declarer then misguessed, misreading our problem, we would be charmed."

As I left the table I thought it appropriate to comfort my opponents. "When you decided to finesse," I said, "I was charmed. Really charmed."

Our next adventure took place a few tables down the road. This time Coldbottom recognized one of the opponents. "He is," Coldbottom said, "a great student of the law. In the December 1977 *Bridge World*, on page 5, in a forceful letter he set out the proper position for all good citizens. 'It is proper and ethical,' he said, 'to pursue one's own interest within the law.' Be careful how you behave," continued Coldbottom, "or you may find yourself involved with the gendarmes."

This was the second deal (swung around for convenience).

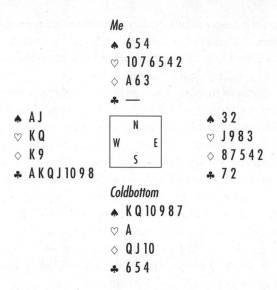

Me
- ♠ 6 5 4
- ♡ 10 7 6 5 4 2
- ◇ A 6 3
- ♣ —

♠ A J   ♠ 3 2
♡ K Q   ♡ J 9 8 3
◇ K 9   ◇ 8 7 5 4 2
♣ A K Q J 10 9 8   ♣ 7 2

Coldbottom
- ♠ K Q 10 9 8 7
- ♡ A
- ◇ Q J 10
- ♣ 6 5 4

After a spirited auction, Coldbottom became declarer in six spades doubled. The opening lead was the ace of clubs. Coldbottom ruffed, came to his hand with a heart, ruffed a club, ruffed a heart and ruffed his last club. With no safe way back to his hand, he announced (he alone having noticed) that dummy was short one card. A frantic search discovered it nestled under my chair. It was the three of clubs.

The director explained that since dummy cannot revoke there could be no penalty. The card lost must be restored to dummy and put in play. Having ruffed three clubs in dummy, Coldbottom now ruffed one back to his hand, put down the king of spades and, as you can see, made his contract.

This typical example of the law in action seemed to depress our opponents. Probably they had been having a good game. Coldbottom tried to cheer them up.

"In my unenlightened days, I would not have played that last club. I would have felt less than a man taking advantage of a situation created by my partner's clumsiness. Thanks to people like you my attitude has changed. Even when the law is an ass it must be obeyed... all the time. However, should you start a movement to repeal this law, you can count on my firm support."

Our third encounter of a strange kind came at the final table. By this stage, I estimated we were within striking range of winning it all. Again Coldbottom recognized one of the opponents.

"Be careful," he said. "That player has no respect for the proprieties. His name is Eros Amaral, and playing once in a South American championship final he was involved in a scandalous adventure. Holding a hand of moderate value, he inadvertently opened the bidding one spade on a two-card suit. As a result, his opponents missed their cold game in spades. Amaral stated that if this hand resulted in loss of the event he would insist that it be redealt. He would not let his slip of the tongue govern the result of a hard-fought match. As it turned out, his opponents won the event (by 1 IMP) and it was unnecessary to accept his offer. In those days, both the magazine and the reporter seemed to approve of this kind of misguided chivalry. 'He showed the whole world,' said David Berah (*The Bridge World*, Feb. 1967, page 35), 'that there is something more important than the desire to win: decency in losing.' Keep your eye on him," Coldbottom continued. "We don't want any repetition of that kind of behavior."

Again, the second hand was crucial.

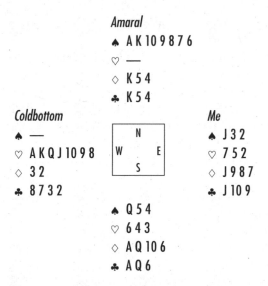

Amaral
♠ A K 10 9 8 7 6
♡ —
◊ K 5 4
♣ K 5 4

Coldbottom
♠ —
♡ A K Q J 10 9 8
◊ 3 2
♣ 8 7 3 2

Me
♠ J 3 2
♡ 7 5 2
◊ J 9 8 7
♣ J 10 9

♠ Q 5 4
♡ 6 4 3
◊ A Q 10 6
♣ A Q 6

Amaral opened one spade, his partner bid two diamonds. Coldbottom jammed with four hearts. Five hearts from Amaral, six clubs from South and now six hearts by Amaral. It was a magnificent bid: a grand-slam force in two suits, with the assurance that the hand was playable at a small slam in spades. Unfortunately, it was not all this clear to South. He pondered and pondered and then, as ponderers are wont to do, he passed. My God! They were about to play slam in our suit!

I pulled out the seven of hearts to make my face-down lead, when it dawned on me that the auction was not over yet. Coldbottom had not passed. He too was pondering. Finally he got the word out. "Double."

Amaral smiled his thanks, corrected to spades and chalked up his slam and, as it turned out, the tournament.

After all this we wound up fifth. Had we played the last hand in six hearts we would have finished second. Suddenly we were confronted by an angry duo. It was the pair who did end up in second place. Had it not been for Coldbottom's gallantry, they would have been first.

"No one gave *us* any second chances," they shouted. Coldbottom was not impressed.

"There is indeed a conflict here," he said. "Your right to win is in conflict with my self-respect. Six months from now, no one will even care who won this event. A man's self-respect, however, once tarnished is forever diminished. What shall it be gentlemen? One bushel of masterpoints, or one shining integrity? It is not whether you win or lose that counts. It is how you answer that question."

The Bridge World Editor's Note (from Edgar Kaplan)

Like Frank Vine, we prize and praise self-respect — but not when it conflicts with law (e.g., when a man's self-respect is such that he habitually challenges to pistols in the morning anyone who has, he fancies, cast a slur on his honor, we want that man locked up, not praised). Once the line between the legal and illegal is crossed, a personal virtue can turn into a crime against society.

Mr. Vine's duplicate bridge with gallantry could be a fair contest only if everyone adhered to the same code (that is, it must be society's code, not just Mr. Vine's), and then only if everyone exercised similar judgments. For example, consider this mix-up we heard recently:

WEST	NORTH	EAST	SOUTH
1NT	pass	2◊¹	2♡²
3♡	dbl	all pass	

1. Transfer to hearts.
2. Takeout.

North, thinking creatively, intended his double as for takeout, since that is what it would have meant on the analogous natural auction: two-heart response by East, takeout double by South, raise by West, responsive double by North. However, South woodenly interpreted the double as for penalty. Well, is this the sort of North-South accident from which a self-respecting East or West should refuse to profit? If not, how does the pass of the double here differ from the pass of the cuebid in Vine's case? And what if the doubled contract happens to go down 200, luckily for North-South — should North, like Amaral in 1967, offer to cancel the board? And should East-West then accept that gracious offer?

Those elegant and courtly questions are difficult to answer, so it is just as well they need not be asked. Organized bridge society has chosen, through its laws, a less chivalrous code. It is illegal for East-West to refuse their score for making three hearts doubled; it is illegal for North-South to cancel their score for setting the contract. If the players find it distasteful to profit through confusion, either the opponents' confusion or their own, they must nonetheless grit their teeth and swallow the profit, putting society's laws above personal notions of good taste even at some cost to self-respect. For an individual to adopt Mr. Vine's knightly code all by himself is antisocial. Like fighting duels today, it is not gallantry but crime.

We trust that few of our readers are "having trouble distinguishing between fighting fierce and fighting foul". The distinction is written down in *The Laws of Duplicate Bridge*. Did you pour ice-water over your 96-year-old opponent, with the chilling effect of getting the poor man to bid out of turn? "*Director!*" He will tell you that he is authorized by Law 77C8 to waive the penalty on request, and that the official ACBL policy is for him to agree to waive whenever the innocent side has helped cause the infraction.

Have you gulled an opponent into a continuation by asking a sly question about the opening lead? Or persuaded an opponent into a losing finesse by an artful four-minute huddle? "Director!" He will say, sharply we hope (Proprieties II, D2), "It is grossly improper to attempt to deceive an opponent by means of remark or gesture, through the haste or hesitancy of a call or play... " Further, there is Proprieties II, F2: "If the Director determines that an innocent opponent has drawn a false inference from deliberately and improperly deceptive information, he should award an adjusted score."

Have you ruffed three times before discovering that dummy had a club on the floor? For heaven's sake, do not improvise your own remedy like Coldbottom in his unenlightened days, who "would have felt less than a man taking advantage... " It is illegal, thus anti-social, for players to deal with infractions on their own. "The responsibility for penalizing irregularities and redressing damage rests solely upon the Director and these Laws, not upon the players themselves," the Proprieties say, testily. So, "Director!"

He will tell you that, although there is no penalty for a revoke from a faced hand, he is specifically instructed (Law 64C) to adjust the score so as to compensate your opponents for damage caused by any unpenalized revoke. Perhaps there is something to be said after all for respecting the laws, which will do a pretty good job if only you let them.

COLDBOTTOM: ON BEING TRUSTWORTHY

One of my favorite movies of all time is The Cincinnati Kid — *for those of you who haven't seen it, it's a stud poker version of* The Hustler. *The incomparable Edward G. Robinson is "The Man", the reigning king of the green baize; Steve McQueen is the young upstart who is sure he can beat him. I won't spoil the movie for you if you haven't seen it, but towards the end, Robinson gets to utter one of my favorite lines: "The art of playing cards is doing the wrong thing at the right time." Professor Coldbottom understands that you have to play your opponents as well as the cards: that bridge is a four-person game, not a two-person game. Watch as he puts The Man's advice into action.*

"You can lie to your parole board, you can lie to the government, you can even lie to your mother, but you must never lie to your partner.

"The key word is discipline. Ah discipline! Hallowed be thy name. It is the rock on which all great partnerships are built. Ultimately, it is the rock on which they founder."

The speaker was Professor Cornelius Coldbottom, the finest player in the game, often the unluckiest. The occasion was that period of quiet just before the final quarter of the knockout championships at Cayuga, the bridge capital of the world. Year after year, we came there to fight for the famed Chicken Roost Trophy, and, as always, our backs were to the wall. Those perennial champions, the Blue Team from Stoney Creek, were mashing us up again. There we were, sixteen boards left to play and 60 IMPs behind. We talked of a comeback, but in our hearts we knew it was all over. Except for Coldbottom.

"In these final boards," he continued, "I will attempt to apply the principle of transverse trust." He gazed at me directly. "Just don't get in my way." Finishing the last of the warm cucumber sandwiches, we returned to battle.

The Coldbottom attack began with the third board. West was Benito Yardstick, who held this hand,

♠ 4 3 2 ♡ 4 3 2 ◊ A J 10 ♣ 5 4 3 2

This was the auction.

WEST	NORTH	EAST	SOUTH
Yardstick	*Me*	*Omar Bellaroma*	*Coldbottom*
			1♠
pass	2◇	pass	3♡
pass	4NT	pass	5◇
dbl	6NT	pass	7♠
all pass			

Benito had heard me bid diamonds, and had doubled vigorously for a diamond lead. The whole world knew he held the ace, and still Coldbottom had gone to seven. Only a cretin would bang down the ace; and Yardstick, no cretin, started a trump. It was not the killing lead.

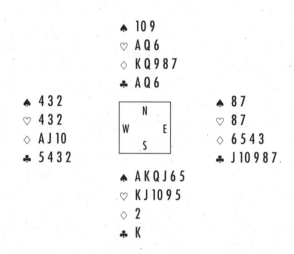

The opponents were furious. Like most of us they held certain truths to be inviolate. You ask for aces, partner answers his aces, and since you live or die by that information, partner never lies. To go to seven, flagrantly, knowing you are off an ace, is completely unacceptable. It is just not done.

A few deals later, Coldbottom showed that he had not changed his ways.

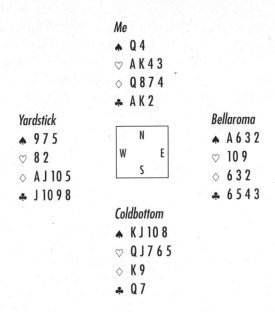

Me
- ♠ Q 4
- ♡ A K 4 3
- ◇ Q 8 7 4
- ♣ A K 2

Yardstick
- ♠ 9 7 5
- ♡ 8 2
- ◇ A J 10 5
- ♣ J 10 9 8

Bellaroma
- ♠ A 6 3 2
- ♡ 10 9
- ◇ 6 3 2
- ♣ 6 5 4 3

Coldbottom
- ♠ K J 10 8
- ♡ Q J 7 6 5
- ◇ K 9
- ♣ Q 7

This is how we bid it.

Coldbottom	Me
2♡[1]	2NT[2]
3♣[3]	4NT[4]
5◇[5]	6♡[6]
pass	

1. Flannery (four spades, five hearts, 12-15 points).
2. Show me your shape.
3. I have a singleton diamond.
4. And do you have any aces?
5. Just one.
6. With confidence.

Coldbottom lied all over the place: about his shape, about his aces. His insanity worked out just fine. Benito led the jack of clubs. This went around to the queen, and a small diamond came out. Benito saw no need to play his ace. After all, declarer's hand was an open book. The ten of diamonds would be the best play. No, it was not.

When the diamond queen held, Coldbottom drew trumps, threw a diamond on the good clubs, conceded the ace of spades, and claimed.

This time the opponents weren't furious, they were apoplectic. Deciding that discretion was best for the moment, I didn't try to soothe their feelings. Besides, if Coldbottom tried to dip his toe into the well again, the opponents were ready for him. The match, however, had tightened up considerably. By the time we reached the last board, it was anybody's guess as to who was leading. Coldbottom went to the whip again.

This was our bidding.

WEST	NORTH	EAST	SOUTH
Yardstick	Me	Bellaroma	Coldbottom
			2NT
pass	3♣	pass	pass(!)

With a sneer in the Professor's direction, Yardstick balanced with a double. Coldbottom was not about to fool him with that old chestnut. Given the circumstances, the decision was a reasonable one. The circumstances, however, were not what most of us thought. Yardstick may just never balance again. These were the four hands; East-West were vulnerable:

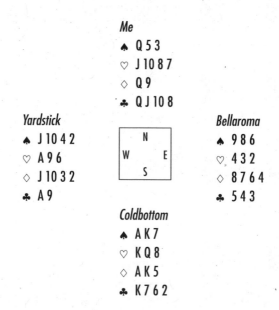

Me
♠ Q 5 3
♡ J 10 8 7
◇ Q 9
♣ Q J 10 8

Yardstick
♠ J 10 4 2
♡ A 9 6
◇ J 10 3 2
♣ A 9

Bellaroma
♠ 9 8 6
♡ 4 3 2
◇ 8 7 6 4
♣ 5 4 3

Coldbottom
♠ A K 7
♡ K Q 8
◇ A K 5
♣ K 7 6 2

Here, Coldbottom had not lied. Not about his shape, not about his points, not about anything. All he had done was pass in a situation where a lesser player might have found a bid. When Bellaroma removed the double to three diamonds, Coldbottom doubled. And that was 1400.

The trip back to Hamilton was a delight. I clutched the Chicken Roost Trophy, and our teammates hummed victory songs. Coldbottom, as usual, sat with his nose buried in a magazine.

"What's that you're reading?" I asked.

"A very interesting article," said Coldbottom. "About a system called Kickback. I think it will adapt very nicely to my new methods."

THE BET

An argument that still rages today: should "anything goes" be the watchword of system legislators, to encourage creativity and advances in bidding theory? Or do weaker or more casual players need protection? And even at the highest levels, is the game well served by allowing what Bobby Wolff calls the products of the "poison gas labs", ideas whose main purpose is destructive rather than constructive? I don't have an answer, but since my own appearances at the table have fallen off to once a year or so, I find myself less and less prepared to work out some defense against Di'Zok overcalls or Rallosian cuebids or whatever else it is I'm going to find if I have the time and inclination to read the fine print on my opponents' card. Three top-level exhibition matches have been played, pitting "Scientists" against "Traditionalists", to determine whether players using very few conventions can do as well or better than players using complex, artificial methods. The Official Encyclopedia of Bridge describes the results as "somewhat inconclusive". Indeed, since the three matches took place in 1965, 1990, and 1992, it's quite possible that the Scientists from the first match were using methods not dissimilar to the Traditionalists in the second and third! And I'm not sure that anyone has ever analyzed the results to determine how many of the IMPs that changed hands were directly attributable to systems as opposed to any of the many other things that can influence the result of any given deal. Ah well, it's differences of opinion that make horse races, as they say.

"I'll bet you $100,000 you're wrong!"

The occasion for this excited outburst was the regular Wednesday-night gathering at the Wentworth Bridge and Social Club, when the big guns meet to dissect the deals played that evening, and to comment on life in general.

Professor Cornelius Coldbottom had been holding court. The subject: artificial systems. "The purpose of a new bridge system," he explained, "is not to improve the accuracy of bidding. It is to confuse the weak and the unwary. Even those few conscientious players who are prepared to devote long boring hours to a study of the intricacies of an opponent's system, in order to prepare a defense, find that as soon as they have done so, two new systems have surfaced. Soon they give up in dismay. Unless someone does something drastic, and soon, duplicate bridge will find itself on the way out, a victim of its seeming inability to yell 'Stop! That's enough!' I will be sad when that happens, since I am convinced that in most situations common-sense bidding is as effective as any artificiality, while the artificial is, in many instances, vulnerable to intelligent subversion."

It was then that young Holly Holliwell, studious, dedicated, and, like most of her generation, a bit of a pain, spoke her challenge.

"I'll bet you $100,000 you're wrong!"

Finally Coldbottom found his voice.

"Do you have $100,000?"

"Well, not really," she admitted, "but I still say I can get a team that will beat the ears off any team of yours. And the reason will be the superiority of our methods."

Surprisingly enough, she found several backers, and after everyone had searched through wallets, the bet was made. Two hundred dollars would be posted by each team, winner take all. Game time would be one week from Thursday, twenty boards to a finish. Once again, the bet was definitely on.

By game time, excitement at the club was at a fever pitch. Everyone understood that the issues at stake were central to our times. It was not just a bridge match. It was youth versus age. The obnoxious versus the self-righteous. The conviction of the young that the established would resist all change, regardless of merit, to protect their own place in the sun. The determination of their elders that radical theories should not sweep away the tried and the true.

In the Closed Room, Omar Bellaroma and Benito Yardstick would sit East-West for the "Neanderthals", as they were now being called. They would play Buller, an austere natural system. For the "Kids" it would be the Sharpie twins, Bill and Phil. They would use a strong-pass system joined to an artificial club and relays.

In the Open Room, jammed with spectators, Coldbottom and Harry Loudmouth took the North-South seats, while Holly Holliwell sat West facing her favorite partner, Felicity Fungus. I managed to scrounge a seat right behind the professor.

The first few boards were even. Then came the first shift in fortune.

Dealer West
East-West vulnerable

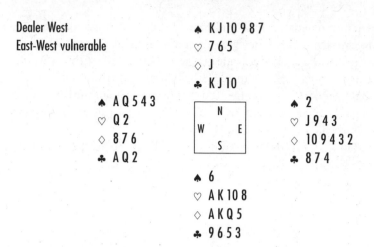

```
                    ♠ K J 10 9 8 7
                    ♡ 7 6 5
                    ◇ J
                    ♣ K J 10
  ♠ A Q 5 4 3            N            ♠ 2
  ♡ Q 2            W         E        ♡ J 9 4 3
  ◇ 8 7 6              S              ◇ 10 9 4 3 2
  ♣ A Q 2                             ♣ 8 7 4
                    ♠ 6
                    ♡ A K 10 8
                    ◇ A K Q 5
                    ♣ 9 6 5 3
```

The Closed Room bidding was what you might expect.

WEST	NORTH	EAST	SOUTH
Bellaroma	Bill	Yardstick	Phil
1♠	pass	pass	dbl
all pass			

Bill Sharpie started a trump, and when the carnage had ended it was North-South plus 1100. A filthy result, but how else could the auction develop?

In the Open Room Holly Holliwell showed them how. As West, she began with a pass! In her system that was 12-15 points and a spade suit. North passed with a sigh, East with relief, and Coldbottom, South, got to open the bidding. He reached game in notrump, stole an extra overtrick, and lost 12 IMPs.

The bulk of the crowd, most of whom had been expecting a slaughter of the innocents (and had made their bets accordingly), stirred uneasily. It was not supposed to go this way. Several boards later they felt a lot worse.

Dealer East
East-West vulnerable

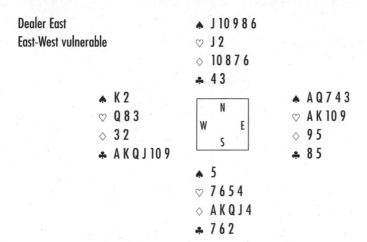

```
                ♠ J 10 9 8 6
                ♡ J 2
                ◇ 10 8 7 6
                ♣ 4 3
♠ K 2                          ♠ A Q 7 4 3
♡ Q 8 3            N           ♡ A K 10 9
◇ 3 2          W     E         ◇ 9 5
♣ A K Q J 10 9     S           ♣ 8 5
                ♠ 5
                ♡ 7 6 5 4
                ◇ A K Q J 4
                ♣ 7 6 2
```

This was the auction in the Closed Room.

WEST	NORTH	EAST	SOUTH
Bellaroma	Bill	Yardstick	Phil
		1♠	2◇
4♣	pass	4♡	pass
4♠	all pass		

It went diamond, diamond, and declarer still had two spades to lose.
Unlucky. But five clubs, of course, was cold.

In the Open Room it went pass (showing spades) – two diamonds –
three clubs, but here Harry Loudmouth, North, the last of the great pre-
emptors, jumped to five diamonds. Fungus passed; Coldbottom passed;
and Holly, unruffled, bid the sixth club. The great leaper found that he had
preempted himself. With zero defense, facing a vulnerable slam, he took
the phantom save. It's called insurance. This time the premium was high,
five down, doubled. That was a further 14 IMPs to the Kids.

By now the supporters of the Neanderthals were in a panic. What
would they tell their friends? How could they face their children? But
Cornelius Coldbottom is not the man to suffer the arrows of misfortune
without firing back. Not long after...

Dealer North
Both sides vulnerable

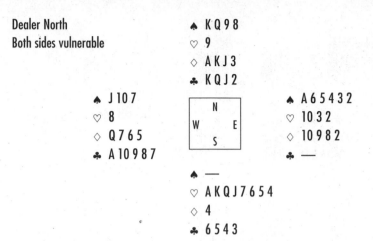

```
                    ♠ K Q 9 8
                    ♡ 9
                    ◇ A K J 3
                    ♣ K Q J 2
    ♠ J 10 7                        ♠ A 6 5 4 3 2
    ♡ 8                             ♡ 10 3 2
    ◇ Q 7 6 5                       ◇ 10 9 8 2
    ♣ A 10 9 8 7                    ♣ —
                    ♠ —
                    ♡ A K Q J 7 6 5 4
                    ◇ 4
                    ♣ 6 5 4 3
```

In the Closed Room Bill Sharpie, North, started with a strong club. South relayed nine times and settled in six hearts. Benito Yardstick, East, had doubled for a club lead, and ace and another club scuttled the contract. It was hard to see how the result could be different in the other room, but Cornelius found a way.

Loudmouth, North, began with one diamond, and Coldbottom, South, aware that the secret of the hand was his partner's club holding, made the practical response of two clubs! "Three hearts," said Loudmouth. Oh God! He had forgotten they were not using any gadgets. He was making a splinter bid.

Coldbottom could see that it was no longer safe to continue scientifically, so he bid what he thought he could make. Seven hearts!

This time it was West who doubled. After all she did hold the ace of clubs. But the splinter bid had put her partner on lead and she didn't have any clubs. She did, however, have the luscious ace of spades and couldn't wait to place it triumphantly on the table. Loudmouth ruffed, drew trumps, finessed against the queen of diamonds, and had all the tricks. That was 21 IMPs back.

A firm believer in the theory of momentum, the professor rammed them again on the very next deal.

Dealer East

East-West vulnerable

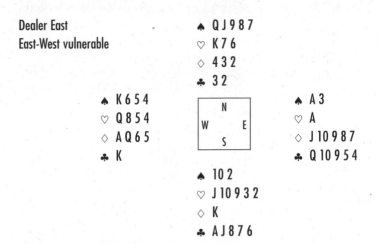

```
                    ♠ Q J 9 8 7
                    ♡ K 7 6
                    ◇ 4 3 2
                    ♣ 3 2

   ♠ K 6 5 4              N              ♠ A 3
   ♡ Q 8 5 4         W         E         ♡ A
   ◇ A Q 6 5              S              ◇ J 10 9 8 7
   ♣ K                                   ♣ Q 10 9 5 4

                    ♠ 10 2
                    ♡ J 10 9 3 2
                    ◇ K
                    ♣ A J 8 7 6
```

Again the Closed Room result was not optimum.

WEST	NORTH	EAST	SOUTH
Bellaroma	Bill	Yardstick	Phil
		1◇	1♡
3NT	pass	4♣	pass
5◇	all pass		

With diamonds friendly, that meant twelve tricks.

Can you get to slam? Not if you're playing Buller, apparently. And not if you're playing fancy either, for this was the auction in the Open Room. East (Felicity): One diamond... Alert! May be very short. Then South (Coldbottom): Two diamonds... Alert! Natural. Shows long diamonds.

Holly, West, had her problems. Her partner held short diamonds. That meant one of two hands: long clubs or two four-card majors. She would like to double if double were negative, but was it? So she chose the unambiguous cuebid. Three diamonds!

Felicity bid an obedient four clubs, Coldbottom passed, and Holly was still not out of the woods. She would like to try four notrump natural. But who plays that? Or four hearts as a further cuebid, but that one could easily be misunderstood. So she abandoned science and a bid a straightforward five clubs.

Strange! You begin by bidding diamonds, partner also bids diamonds, and yet there is no way to play the hand in diamonds. Anyway, five clubs was not a friendly contract. Down two, and 12 IMPs to the Neanderthals. They had taken the lead.

By the time the last board arrived, everyone knew the match was close. What no one knew was that, with this and that happening, it was an exact tie. This deal would decide the outcome.

Dealer East
Both sides vulnerable

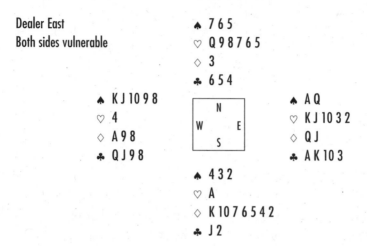

♠ 7 6 5
♡ Q 9 8 7 6 5
◇ 3
♣ 6 5 4

♠ K J 10 9 8
♡ 4
◇ A 9 8
♣ Q J 9 8

♠ A Q
♡ K J 10 3 2
◇ Q J
♣ A K 10 3

♠ 4 3 2
♡ A
◇ K 10 7 6 5 4 2
♣ J 2

In the Closed Room Bellaroma and Yardstick rose smartly to six clubs, plus 1370. It was, in theory, the best contract. Nevertheless, both six spades and six notrump would make. If either were bid in the other room, the Kids would win the match. And they had the system that could do it.

Sure enough, Felicity, East, began with a forcing club.

"One heart," said Coldbottom. This was Alerted and explained as being an exclusion bid. And what was an exclusion bid? It was a takeout of the forcing club, showing shortness in hearts and support for the other three suits.

Holly doubled, negative, thinking, "Wouldn't it be nice if they ended up in spades?" Loudmouth passed, thinking, "Please, God, don't let him bid diamonds." East passed, thinking, "Lovely, they're in my suit!" And Coldbottom? As everyone knows, he doesn't just listen to the bidding, he also listens to the thinking. That's what makes him the professor. He deduced that the only explanation for Loudmouth's pass was a fistful of hearts. More important, this was his last sure chance to control the destiny of the deal. So he passed, Holly led her heart, and East-West took a pile of tricks. But they couldn't stop Coldbottom from making three trump tricks. That was 1100 to East-West; 8 IMPs to North-South; and game, set and match to the Neanderthals.

Well that's the story of the bet. Nothing has changed because of it. Both sides are still convinced they were vindicated. It's what I always say. You can win a war, or the girl of your dreams, but you can never win an argument.

COLDBOTTOM IN FRONT OF THE COMMITTEE

> *Committees are the bane of bridge, and we would all be better off without them. There, I've said it. Their rulings are too arbitrary, too often wrong-headed, and the whole system encourages litigious types to try to get in committee what they have failed to win at the table. It's one of the reasons I retired from the tournament game. And, lest you think the committee's ruling on the Professor's appeal here far-fetched, there was a very similar case in the 2008 Detroit Spring Nationals — a player balanced on essentially a yarborough opposite a hesitating partner, who later turned out to have 20+ HCP. The committee ruled in his favor! The point surely, as the Professor explains, is that the hesitation takes any risk out of the doubtful action. At the time this piece was written, the rules were as Frank describes — if partner huddled, you were allowed to take an action that it was adjudged 80% of your peers would take (now there's a clear-cut legal yardstick). Today, we have progressed(?) to LOLA, the law of logical alternatives. Nowadays, we are not permitted to select from logical alternatives any one that may have been suggested by partner's huddle. It's not clear we are better off — the Detroit committee ruled that the strong hand's huddle did not clearly suggest any particular action. Obviously, it did suggest action as opposed to inaction — and the committee that ruled this way has correctly come in for serious criticism. But of course, in bridge you can't appeal an appeal.*

"It is time," said Cornelius Coldbottom, "to invade America again." His target this time was the Summer Nationals and the Life Master Pairs.

Unfortunately, some would say predictably, none of his regular partners was available. Finally, he made the only deal he could. He would play with Holly Holliwell: young, earnest and *très scientifique*.

As expected, there were a lot of negotiations about conventions. Holly, who considers relay systems simplistic, was appalled at the Coldbottom approach to the game. Her bottom line, a list of conventions she scathingly referred to as "basic bridge for newborn babes", still represented a formidable learning experience for the Professor, who had always placed his trust in Buller, the natural system for natural people.

His cronies at the Wentworth Bridge and Social Club were convulsed.

"About the best that can happen to them," said Harry Loudmouth, "is a catastrophe."

His words seemed prophetic when they sat down to the very first board.

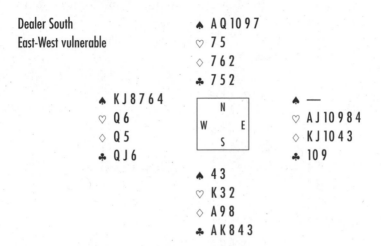

Dealer South
East-West vulnerable

North: ♠ A Q 10 9 7 ♡ 7 5 ◇ 7 6 2 ♣ 7 5 2

West: ♠ K J 8 7 6 4 ♡ Q 6 ◇ Q 5 ♣ Q J 6

East: ♠ — ♡ A J 10 9 8 4 ◇ K J 10 4 3 ♣ 10 9

South: ♠ 4 3 ♡ K 3 2 ◇ A 9 8 ♣ A K 8 4 3

At most tables there was a sameness to the auction. One club by South, a two spade overcall by West, two passes, a reopening double, two more passes, and finally a red-suit rescue by East, invariably successful. At Coldbottom's table things took a twist. Holly began with one club all right, and West overcalled two spades, but Coldbottom, forgetting he was playing negative doubles, said, "Double."

"Alert," said Holly, "the double is takeout"

"Aha," thought East, a cunning sort, "this looks promising. I'll just sit back and wait for them to land in a red suit, then I'll carry them out on a plate."

He failed to reckon with Holly. Despite her youth and studious bent, she was a practical player. As she later explained to the committee, her thinking went something like this: "I can't bid hearts, notrump or diamonds. I'm not strong enough to cuebid, and that leaves only three clubs. Not an appealing choice. But if I pass, I have four tricks almost for sure, and if partner has the decency to produce another two, bingo! It's a chance. But even Mrs. Columbus took a chance."

So Holly passed, and East never got to make his master call, and the number was eleven hundred.

What could the committee do? A "wire" was impossible — this was the very first board. So it had to let the result stand. The chairman, like most of his breed, felt obliged to proffer words of wisdom and advice.

"You have not done anything wrong," he warned, "but the incident will have to be recorded in our files." Coldbottom rather resented that, but since it was unlikely he would be in front of a committee for another twenty years, he let the remark pass.

However, he was back in front of the committee that same day. This was the deal that caused the commotion:

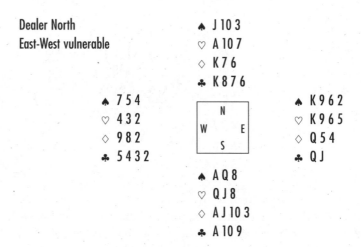

Dealer North
East-West vulnerable

♠ J 10 3
♡ A 10 7
◇ K 7 6
♣ K 8 7 6

♠ 7 5 4
♡ 4 3 2
◇ 9 8 2
♣ 5 4 3 2

♠ K 9 6 2
♡ K 9 6 5
◇ Q 5 4
♣ Q J

♠ A Q 8
♡ Q J 8
◇ A J 10 3
♣ A 10 9

After two passes it was Coldbottom's turn with the South cards. He could see it was a hand with little scope for variety. The bidding would go one something, one something, a jump to two notrump, and North would then place the contract. If he had an edge in play, that would be offset by the defensive skills of his opponents, Saul Klutz and Jordan Shmutz, two famous internationalists. It seemed appropriate to try for a small swing. So Coldbottom conservatively opened the bidding with one notrump.

This was a little swingier than you might think, since, at Holly's insistence, their notrump range was eleven to thirteen points! Perhaps something might happen to justify the euphoria of *The Bridge World* editors. Coldbottom had another thing going for him. He knew from the first board in the round that East was a fearless balancer.

Anyway, West passed, Holly passed, and the fearless balancer, true to the code of Klutz, reopened with a double. "Redouble," said Coldbottom, and he doubled everything after that, including the final contract of two spades which went down seventeen hundred points. It was back to the committee.

At first the committee was inclined to treat the episode as good, clean fun. One inept idiot forgets he's playing the weak notrump and one fellow expert is crucified. It happens all the time. When the Professor made it known that his action had been deliberate, the mood turned sour. Here was a member of the common herd making a monkey of one of their own. How was that going to look to the customers? On the other hand, where was the violation? Certainly Holly had not fielded the psyche. And East! He had been looking at a cold top until he decided on his *very* questionable balance.

Once again the charge was dismissed and once again the chairman started on his caution. This time Coldbottom would have none of it. "If my action was correct," he said, "then you have no comment to make. If my action was not correct, then my partner and I were parties to disreputable behavior and should be charged accordingly. If that is the allegation then state it, and I will instruct my attorney to sue each of you, singly and collectively, for fifty million dollars."

That kind of threat might have been laughed at back in Canada, but in the land of lawyers' delight, where everyone sues at and for the drop of a hat, and where endless lunatic jurors hand out vast sums of someone else's money just because it's there, the threat was very real. The members of the committee were quiet as mice as Coldbottom stalked triumphantly from the courtroom.

For a change, the second day was uneventful, and Holly and the Professor wound their way higher and higher in the standings through the semifinals. But in the first final session this deal came up.

Dealer South
East-West vulnerable

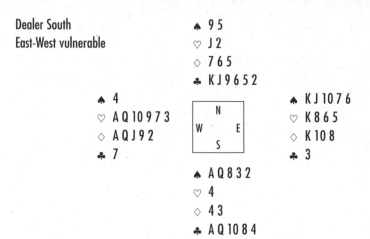

```
                           ♠ 9 5
                           ♡ J 2
                           ◇ 7 6 5
                           ♣ K J 9 6 5 2
        ♠ 4                                    ♠ K J 10 7 6
        ♡ A Q 10 9 7 3          N              ♡ K 8 6 5
        ◇ A Q J 9 2        W         E         ◇ K 10 8
        ♣ 7                      S             ♣ 3
                           ♠ A Q 8 3 2
                           ♡ 4
                           ◇ 4 3
                           ♣ A Q 10 8 4
```

Coldbottom, South, faced a classical dilemma. Some, let us call them sons of Kaplan, like to open this hand one spade. They think the important thing is to preempt and get the spades shown. Others, let's call them the bulk of the world, open the bidding one club. This makes for an easier, smoother auction. It also allows an easier, smoother entry for the opponents. Often, the spade suit is lost unless the opener is willing to introduce it at a suicide level. Coldbottom is a follower of *both* camps! Sometimes he goes for the spade bid and sometimes he opens one club. On this occasion he felt, for sundry reasons, that preemption was paramount, and so he opened the hand... one heart!

This was not pleasing to West, but all he could do was pass. Holly bid one forcing notrump. Now Coldbottom completed the picture of his hand: Two diamonds! When Holly gave him a preference to two hearts, Coldbottom knew her whole hand. She had at most three spades, at most two hearts and at most three diamonds. Her longest suit had to be clubs and it was five to seven cards long. If so, the opponents were cold for a vulnerable game in one of the red suits. But only if he gave them a chance to bid it! Coldbottom passed, and there was West. Tied to the mast. He couldn't double — partner would take out to a black suit. Anyway, he thought it might not be too bad defending. When the hands don't fit, any plus is welcome. Alas, the plus was larger than he wanted, as Coldbottom managed to snag just two tricks. That was 300 for East-West, a clear zero.

Once again they were back in the halls of jurisprudence. The protest seems frivolous, but nowadays the world is replete with those who take every bad result to arbitration. Who knows how many lunatic jurors may be sitting as adjudicators? The committee members were a bit testier this time. Coldbottom was becoming notorious. They couldn't pin anything on him, and that was making them nervous. They felt his tactics had no right to be so successful. After all, he wasn't even a professional. But what could they do? He had psyched and the opponents had failed to cope. So where was the crime?

"Do you psyche like this often at home?" one member asked.

"Only when my opponent begs for it," said Coldbottom. "On the first deal of the set, holding a balanced hand with eight points West sat there yawning, barely glancing at his hand. This time he sat on the edge of his seat, his eyes glued to the cards. I made a calculation based on his mannerisms. As a matter of fact, his actions were quite an overbid. His hand was not nearly that strong. Had I been wrong, had he again held a balanced eight-count, then I would be the one getting the bottom. One thing I assure you. Had that been the case, I would have accepted the loss without coming whining to you." Once more he left the room with head held high.

There was to be one final confrontation. But this time the complainant was Coldbottom. It was a drama at high midnight. Our heroes had gone into the last board leading the field. Even an average on this board would ensure them the title.

These were the cards:

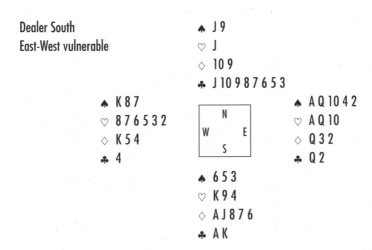

Dealer South
East-West vulnerable

♠ J 9
♡ J
♢ 10 9
♣ J 10 9 8 7 6 5 3

♠ K 8 7
♡ 8 7 6 5 3 2
♢ K 5 4
♣ 4

♠ A Q 10 4 2
♡ A Q 10
♢ Q 3 2
♣ Q 2

♠ 6 5 3
♡ K 9 4
♢ A J 8 7 6
♣ A K

Coldbottom, South, started with one diamond; West passed; Holly bid one notrump (not forcing over a minor); and East... well, he stroked his beard and rubbed his nose and stared at the stars and finally passed. Coldbottom also passed, and West promptly bid two hearts. Holly passed to see what she would see, and two hearts became the final contract.

Minus 170 was a terrible score for the Hamilton pair. East-West can make game in either major, but if they bid it North will surely bid five clubs, down only one after the normal heart lead. If one notrump is allowed to play, it will be down 150.

The director ruled that the two-heart bid could stand, and an irate Coldbottom immediately appealed the decision. The courtroom and the surrounding corridor were jammed. By this time everyone knew the importance of the deal. Besides, Coldbottom was now somewhat of a celebrity. The entire judiciary committee was on hand. They made short shrift of the appeal. As the chairman put it:

"There was a hesitation. No doubt of that. But West's bid of two hearts was virtually automatic. It is a bid that 80% of West's peers would make 75% of time, in the absence of a hesitation by their partner. West is an expert. So are the members of this committee. And every one of us would bid with his cards, huddle or no huddle."

"Gentlemen," said Coldbottom, "you are right and I was wrong. Any reasonable player would bid two hearts. After all, partner should be marked with some cards. Mind you, there would be a risk. North and South could each be at the top range of their bids, and opener might hold four strong hearts even in a one-diamond bid. But taking a chance is part of the game. I brought this matter to your attention because I felt that this particular West had not been taking that risk. The hesitation by his partner had removed it.

"Now I can see I was in error. West had every right to bid. The rules you so clearly express permit him to do so, and it is his duty to fight as hard as he can for advantage within the rules. I believe there are those who consider that to be the very essence of sportsmanship. Ethical conduct is thus defined in mathematical terms and is divorced from moral judgment. Some enlightened day that method will be applied to other areas of life. What a triumph for justice when a bank robber, charged with the slaying of a bank teller, is judged by what 80% of other bank robbers would do in the given situation.

"May I congratulate my opponents? You are true bridge champions, and, to me, scoundrels of the first rank." With that, Coldbottom made his final exit from the committee room. For a time Holly and the Professor walked along in silence. Finally, Holly spoke.

"Cornelius," she said, "May I ask you a favor of you?"

"Of course, Holly, what is it you wish?"

"I would like you to teach me to play Buller."

COLDBOTTOM PLAYED PRO

I understand that there isn't enough money in bridge for even most of the elite to make their living playing it, winning prize money and collecting fat endorsement checks as they do in other sports. But it bothers me to see world championships being contested and even won by teams carrying paying sponsors who are very average players. It bothers me even more when the bridge press treats the sponsors as though they really are world championship caliber. Imagine the reaction if sponsors got to buy a place on a Ryder Cup team, for example, or enough money would get you a few innings in right field for the Yankees. Meanwhile, in the lower reaches of tournaments, the pros are just trying to win their clients a few masterpoints in the KOs or the Swiss, like our hero in this story. What happens at the table becomes an exercise in manipulation — the pro plays "Guess the Contract" in the auction, and does everything possible to spare the client the pressure of being declarer or having to find a tough defense. Everything becomes a crapshoot. To paraphrase Marshal Bosquet's comment on the Charge of the Light Brigade, "C'est magnifique, mais ce n'est pas le bridge." And personally, if I want to shoot craps, I'll go to Las Vegas, not to a bridge tournament.

Where were you when the plaster hit the fan? They'll be asking that one when the leaves have turned to rust. Because that is how the whole shooting match started. The plaster in question, descending from the ceiling, drifted into the fan swirling just below, and splattered everyone in the Wentworth Bridge and Social Club. The hollering went on for days, but the problem had been there for months. The premises were unbecoming.

What could we do? Borrow? Not when our deficit was high enough to worry Ronald Reagan. Raise dues? Who would swallow that? Harry Loudmouth, our economic specialist, proposed a supply-side solution.

"There's a Regional coming up in Atlanta," he said. "I know a couple of rich palookas who would be delighted to dish out a lotta bucks just to be on a team with the famous Cornelius Coldbottom. I'll be the fourth, and whatever we make goes to fixing up the club rooms."

We were all for it — someone else to do the dirty work, all of us to benefit. What could be fairer than that? Coldbottom did not see it that way. Play for pay was an affront to his image of himself. I argued him down. "Prostitution for one weekend is better than plaster raining on your head for the rest of the year," I said. That did it.

Loudmouth spent a lot of hours coaching him. "Remember," he warned, "it's not pointers they're after. It's masterpoints. So bite your tongue and paint a smile on your face. You are not going to come first. Forget about that! Your aim is to win a few matches — even that won't be easy."

After losing four matches with Monica Moneybags, Coldbottom could see that point. If there was a way to mangle the hand, she found it. With thirty victory points available per round, their total stood at forty-one.

The dinner hour was glum, but, while the others relived the hands, the Professor searched for a new approach. So began Coldbottom's march through Georgia.

The first board set the tone.

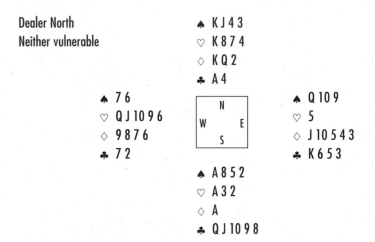

Dealer North
Neither vulnerable

North:
♠ K J 4 3
♡ K 8 7 4
◇ K Q 2
♣ A 4

West:
♠ 7 6
♡ Q J 10 9 6
◇ 9 8 7 6
♣ 7 2

East:
♠ Q 10 9
♡ 5
◇ J 10 5 4 3
♣ K 6 5 3

South:
♠ A 8 5 2
♡ A 3 2
◇ A
♣ Q J 10 9 8

With North starting one notrump, it is normal to reach six spades. With trumps foul and the club king wrong, that is one down. The opponents got to the better six notrump at Loudmouth's table, but that too was one short. Monica also started with one notrump. By now, there was no way Coldbottom would allow her to play a slam. Yet the cards were too good to settle for game. So he made the practical professional bid — six clubs! Just try to beat it. Two spades go on the diamonds, and one ruff sets up the suit. It's the kind of result that destroys enemy morale, and that was blitz number one for the good guys.

The next match was also decided on the first board.

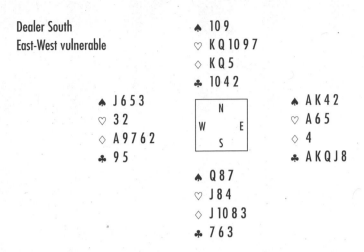

Dealer South
East-West vulnerable

North
♠ 10 9
♡ K Q 10 9 7
◇ K Q 5
♣ 10 4 2

West
♠ J 6 5 3
♡ 3 2
◇ A 9 7 6 2
♣ 9 5

East
♠ A K 4 2
♡ A 6 5
◇ 4
♣ A K Q J 8

South
♠ Q 8 7
♡ J 8 4
◇ J 10 8 3
♣ 7 6 3

Six spades is a delight. You win the heart lead, play two high spades, then pitch your losers on the good clubs. Loudmouth bid it nicely. After two passes, North opened one heart; Loudmouth, East, doubled, and, when his partner answered two diamonds, he cuebid two hearts. When partner admitted to the spade suit, Harry put him right into six.

But how do you get to spades when South opens the bidding one spade? West passed, Monica tried one forcing notrump, and East contested with a double. Over two diamonds by West, Monica introduced the hearts. After all, her partner had opened the bidding. East believed it all (why not?) and took his shot at three notrump. Put Wolff and Hamman East-West, let them be advised by Belladonna, and I still suspect the result would be the same. When an opponent picks off your suit, you lose the four-four fit. That's life. The Coldbottom psyche triggered a collapse, and the team had its second blitz. Suddenly, they were over average.

Match number three belonged to Monica.

Dealer North
North-South vulnerable

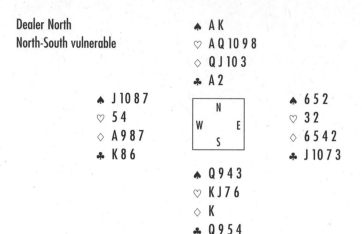

♠ A K
♡ A Q 10 9 8
◇ Q J 10 3
♣ A 2

♠ J 10 8 7
♡ 5 4
◇ A 9 8 7
♣ K 8 6

♠ 6 5 2
♡ 3 2
◇ 6 5 4 2
♣ J 10 7 3

♠ Q 9 4 3
♡ K J 7 6
◇ K
♣ Q 9 5 4

Sedated by events, Cornelius raised Monica's heart opening to three, and she bulled right into six. East, the last of the cunning leaders, started the three of clubs. It is probably right to fly with the queen, but Monica, who couldn't conceive of anyone underleading a king against slam, resigned herself to defeat; she put in the nine. West, not one to give up the ghost, played low, and Monica, all set to win with the ace, played it anyhow. Now she pulled trumps, and followed with the king of diamonds. In with the ace, West saw no merit in playing the king of clubs when declarer was marked with a singleton. He tried a spade, only to see all the club losers in dummy disappear on the diamonds. It was the ultimate Grosvenor. As Frederick Turner foresaw in creating his monster, there is nothing quite like it for driving victims berserk. They pitched IMPs like confetti, and the good guys had blitzed again.

That, by itself, would have been enough. Monica and her financial partner had achieved the supreme moment of the customer. Their names were on the leader board. What bliss to roam in front of it and comment audibly on the various possibilities for final placement, making sure everyone knew it was they up there!

The last match was not about to be a picnic. These were formidable opponents, not easily shaken. Nevertheless, everyone in this world does have his shaky moments, as the Professor was about to demonstrate.

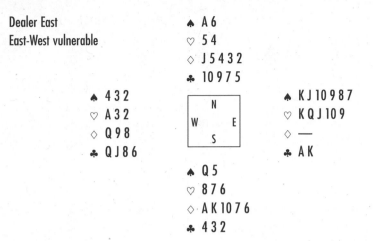

Dealer East
East-West vulnerable

♠ A 6
♡ 5 4
◇ J 5 4 3 2
♣ 10 9 7 5

♠ 4 3 2
♡ A 3 2
◇ Q 9 8
♣ Q J 8 6

N
W E
S

♠ K J 10 9 8 7
♡ K Q J 10 9
◇ —
♣ A K

♠ Q 5
♡ 8 7 6
◇ A K 10 7 6
♣ 4 3 2

Six spades is great because everything sits favorably. You ruff the opening lead, go to your *one* dummy entry in hearts, and lead a trump: putting up the king is clearly right. It all works like a charm.

But what do you do when things *don't* sit nicely — when South leads a small trump to the ace, and a trump comes back? You do exactly what this declarer did. You go down.

These were not the kind of opponents who fold over one deal. Coldbottom understood that. He would have to gull them at least one more time. The third deal provided the chance.

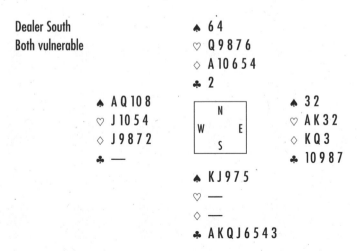

Dealer South
Both vulnerable

♠ 6 4
♡ Q 9 8 7 6
◇ A 10 6 5 4
♣ 2

♠ A Q 10 8
♡ J 10 5 4
◇ J 9 8 7 2
♣ —

N
W E
S

♠ 3 2
♡ A K 3 2
◇ K Q 3
♣ 10 9 8 7

♠ K J 9 7 5
♡ —
◇ —
♣ A K Q J 6 5 4 3

How do you handle the South hand? Who can be dogmatic? Against Loudmouth, South began one club, certainly sensible. North-South now bid one heart, two spades, two notrump, three spades, four spades. There followed a sporting double from West. South ran to the safety of his long suit. Wrong! That was two down instead of one.

The Professor also started sensibly. Pass! It was East who got to open the bidding one club. Now came a typical Coldbottom decision. Double! No doubt he was planning something crafty for later, but his double was followed by three dubious decisions. Redouble from West, a bit light, but with lust in his heart; pass by Monica, intending to bid a lot later on; and pass by East, with perfect faith in Bridge World Standard, 1984. The only clear-cut action was the Professor's final pass. That was not in the least dubious. 2200!

A fourth straight blitz meant that the team had scored a monumental 120 Victory Points on the last four matches, enough to snatch a third-place finish. Coldbottom went home with Monica's promise to see him at the Canadian Nationals ringing in his ears.

Will he take her up on it? Normally I'd guess no, but they do say that, once you play pro, it's hard to break the habit.

Comment

AN OLD APPROACH

> *Convention proliferation is just as much, if not more, of a problem to modern players as it was to those of the 1970s and 1980s. There are certainly many today who, as Frank did back then, feel that more stringent controls are essential if bridge is ever to have any hope of attracting the kind of popular attention currently enjoyed by poker (which is where it is partly due to its inherent simplicity). Watching poker is like watching top-level golf: we may not be able to do what the pros do, but it's sure easy to understand the issues. Bridge isn't like that, unfortunately, although perhaps it should be. The other side of the argument is that this approach would retard progress in bidding theory. In any case, a good bidding system must obstruct the opponents bidding, as well as provide a constructive framework for your side. Frank's point, however, is that if the trend isn't reversed, there may not be many tournament bridge players left in another twenty years.*

Twenty years ago, at Hamilton, I played in my first bridge tournament. My partner and I came fourth in a field of nearly one hundred tables. Twenty years later you might expect that the entries would be twice that, considering all the people who have started playing duplicate bridge since then. But no. During the last ten years Hamilton has been lucky to attract forty tables to an Open Pairs. It is the same story all over the place. The recent Nationals in Chicago (*1980 — Ed.*) had the lowest turnout in years. And the rot continues.

One villain is certainly inflation. Never again will we see the corned beef and pastrami extravaganzas presided over by a smiling Leo Takefman that used to follow the Toronto sectionals. Another problem is too many tournaments. Still that does not explain why so many people who used to attend religiously no longer play in anything. So I asked around and here is what I heard.

"Tournaments are just not fun anymore. We sit down at a table to be confronted by a ton of conventions, most of which we have never heard. We're not students of the game. We came to play and have some fun. Bridge is supposed to be skill and flair, but today you have to read a dozen books or play every other day just to keep up. What's worse, is that the conventions seem designed not for bidding, but to confuse anyone who hasn't had a chance to study them, or to intimidate the less experienced players. And the people in charge either don't care enough to stop it or lack the guts."

Are they right? Well, here's what happened to me at the last Toronto tournament.

♠ Q 8 4
♡ K 5
◇ A K 9 8 6
♣ J 6 4

♠ 2
♡ A Q J 4
◇ 4 2
♣ A K 10 8 7 3

The slam is based more on fit than power, and to be reached intelligently, requires visualizing partner's probable distribution consistent with his bidding. Well, at the table I came to, the opponent's convention card read like this:

> Opening bids other than one club — 4 to 10 points.
> Takeout doubles — zero to fourteen points; with shape 15 to 18
>   points balanced.
> Notrump range — different in different positions.

There was lots of similar stuff on both sides of the page. I asked if they had the permission of the director to play this system. I was told that they did as long as they alerted everything.

Now wasn't that generous! Were this a knockout IMP match I could demand all the time I needed to study the card and work out some defenses. But at an Open Pairs, with fifteen minutes available to play two boards and being constantly reminded by the director that bridge is a timed event, the realistic time available is about ten seconds. Compare this to the hours and days the opponents have spent formulating this system and discussing the ramifications of every bid and you can see how fair it is.

Well, anyhow, the auction began. I started with one diamond, North doubled, East redoubled and South bid one heart. After that it was all a crap-shoot, until my partner finally guessed well and bid the slam. So why am I griping? Because I came to play bridge and not to shoot craps. Because I had none of the satisfaction or pleasure that comes with bidding a hand nicely. What's more, despite my average plus, I was happy to leave that table, and next time, sooner than play there again, I'll probably decide to stay home.

Most people are basically sensible. Beat them with a nice play, a sharp defense, or a well thought-out bid, and they may not grin, but they'll accept it as part of the game. But let them feel jobbed, or cheated, or made a fool of and they may just decide to take their entertainment dollar some other place.

So what does the establishment do about it? They stand aside and let the blood seep on the floor. Every day another car-load of conventions comes in and faced by The Lust Club, The Lebovic Diamond, and similar "I'm out to grab you" systems, the average player says, "Who needs it?", and doesn't come back.

Well, what do I think should be done? First I would start in on the conventions. As someone who has invented a few in the past, I stand, not on the side of the lovers of freedom but rather with people like Don Oakie and the so-called old guard, who have the good common sense to realize that the game is being strangled to death. I would convene a meeting of qualified people to carefully weed through and prune the present allowable conventions and strike out at least one third. Then I would do the same with systems. I would say, for instance, you wish to play a club system? Fine. Then you play either Precision or Blue Team and that's it. No Roman, no Schenken, no New South Wales. After that no new conventions and no new systems. Then after ten years we would take another look. What about the people who can't live without exercising their inventiveness? Well they can argue their case... every tenth year.

TO THE EDITOR OF THE KIBITZER

As we saw in "Coldbottom in Front of the Committee", commit-
tees in bridge can be problematic. Indeed, given their position to
change the outcome long after play has ended, I believe they are
a phenomenon unique to bridge. After all, this isn't a video
replay to determine whether a ball or a puck crossed a line —
this is a post-mortem examination of suggestions, inferences and
motivations, often in situations where the most ethical player in
the world has no idea what his rights or responsibilities are.
Small wonder that bridge committees have come up with some
spectacularly bad decisions. But just because they don't rule
your way doesn't automatically mean that you got hosed. Here
Frank Vine puts on his lawyer's persona and lets one litigant
have it with both barrels.

In your last issue there was a letter from James Hardy which deserves comment. He tells a harrowing story. Holding 23 high card points and cold for
game in two suits, he has his opponents misinform him (and each other)
about the meaning of one of their systemic bids, and he and his partner lan-
guish in a partial.

The case went to a committee of "name" players who ruled against Mr.
Hardy and he argues that such committees should not be composed mere-
ly of top players (who don't understand the problems of the little man) but
should also contain a sprinkling of average players. He cites as a precedent
the jury system, which as we all know bars all legal experts from service.

Well Mr. Hardy, I have been in the law business a long time and have
yet to meet anyone in the trade who has the slightest belief that the jury
system leads to justice. Don't get me wrong. Lawyers love juries. Give
yourself an absolutely stinking case, with the law and facts dead against you,
and you still stand a good chance of finding at least one baboon out of
twelve jurors who is ready to swallow any drivel. The same principle applies
to bridge committees. The questions involved are generally complex. It
takes people with a wide knowledge of all aspects of the game to arrive at
an equitable decision. In one way you are quite right. Had there been people of lesser experience judging your case you might indeed have been given
another decision, but that is only because you were wrong, Mr. Hardy, dead
wrong.

You see, it is not a rule that you get something for nothing every time your opponents break a bridge law. Most times you must still show that you were damaged by the infraction. In your particular case the bad result did not come from bad behavior. It came from bad bridge.

In the first place, you were hurt by your chosen system. The strong club may have its virtues, but it is the easiest of the strong openings for the opponents to jam, as they did here. Secondly, at your first opportunity to describe your hand you underbid by a full ace. Despite all this, you were given another chance and wound up in three notrump, which was going to make, no doubt about it, on the marked spade lead. Unhappily, your partner pulled to four of a minor, and this without being doubled, thus ignoring the first rule of winning bridge: Don't run until the shooting starts. All this made the final result the fault of your partnership and there is no question that the committee ruled correctly.

While I am on the subject of committees, let me say this. Your average player would not be happy serving on one. You give up a good part of your dinner hour, you miss most of the festivities following the game, you work energetically to come to a fair, impartial and just decision, giving full weight, Mr. Hardy, to the level of experience of the players involved in each instance, and in return you get no pay, little thanks, and make a lot of enemies. Not to mention the abuse you receive from certain poor losers who spend the next few weeks taking carefully laundered versions of the facts to anyone who will listen and scream about the rooking they got from the committee. As you can see, I think it is about time someone talked back.

BRIDGE IS A SOLO SPORT

The original title of this piece was Bridge is a Separatist Game. *Since the article came from a Canadian writer, I naturally assumed this was some kind of reference to Quebec's ambitions for independence, but gradually it dawned on me that the allusion was to the classic Al Roth – Tobias Stone book,* Bridge is a Partnership Game. *Deciding that if I was confused, others might also be, I have exercised editorial prerogative and given it a new title. Je m'excuse.*

There is one quality no self-respecting bridge player will admit he lacks, and that is *discipline*. Call him a dummy mangler, tell him he defends like a goat — he'll only grin and bear it. Suggest, however, that he is short on discipline and he will spit in your eye. The reason is simple. Confronted at the table by an avalanche of systems and conventions, the average player finds that only the grimmest totalitarianism will keep the structure of partnership afloat. The dictum of Roth and Stone that "Bridge is a Partnership Game" is the one facet of their philosophy that has never been questioned. Until now, that is. I now question it.

Certain peculiar things have been happening to me at the bridge table. I keep doing the right theoretical things and keep getting the wrong practical results. At first I chalked it up to bad luck; now I'm beginning to think it might just be bad upbringing. To test my theory I have devised this little quiz. You will be given the exact situations I met at the table, and the scoring will be wholly pragmatic. If you would have done well at the table you will do well here — and vice-versa.

The first hand is at matchpoints. You are playing a form of the Roman two diamonds in which that opening can show a hand of 17 high-card points or better, divided specifically 4-4-4-1. Responder must bid two hearts and opener then shows where his singleton is by bidding it. After that, the responder places the final contract. The opener is allowed to bid again only if he holds a super monster.

A burly character on your left passes and partner opens with a bid of two diamonds. The next player, a surly type, twitches slightly, and passes. You hold, vulnerable against non-vulnerable:

♠ 5 4 ♡ 8 7 6 ♢ 8 7 ♣ 8 7 6 5 4 3

For 25 points,
1. You bid two hearts and if partner bids three clubs, showing a singleton, you pass. If his singleton is elsewhere, you propose to bid four clubs.
2. Same as above except that you will bid three hearts if partner shows a singleton club.
3. Same as above except that you will jump to five if partner has clubs.
4. Some other action. Please specify.

For a further 25 points,
1. You are enchanted to be playing the convention. You have a feeling that you are going to reach a magic spot the rest of the field won't come close to.
2. You are mildly worried. After all, you don't hold too many high cards.
3. You are sick to the stomach.

The second hand came up in an IMP game. You are playing negative doubles through three spades, together with an iron-clad agreement with your partner that when there has been an opening bid, an overcall, and a pass, the opener must balance. You even have it written on your card. This time both sides are vulnerable. Your hand is:

♠ A Q 6 4 2   ♡ 10 9   ◇ A 6 5   ♣ Q 9 8

You are the dealer and you open one spade. Left-hand opponent, a timid-looking lady, overcalls two hearts. Both partner and the opponent, another timid-looking lady, pass.

For 25 points, do you
1. Double, on the theory that if you were playing penalty doubles and partner had hit the overcall, you were going to sit for it?
2. Bid two spades?
3. Some other action? Please specify.

For a second 25 points,
1. You are pleased to be playing negative doubles on this hand. You have the feeling that a nice number is just around the corner.
2. You expect the result would have been the same irrespective of what kind of double you were playing.
3. You are sick to the stomach.

Answers

The first hand came up in a Regional Men's Pairs game. I held the hand in question and when it came my turn to bid I admit to feeling a trifle apprehensive (10 points), but as I bid two hearts I couldn't help thinking that if partner held just the right cards we might even have a slam (minus 5 points). Over my two hearts Burly passed, partner bid three clubs (what else?), and Surly came out into the open with a double. Now I got sick to the stomach (25 points). I had been proposing to pass a three-club bid (10 points), but when the double came in, I decided to squirm to three hearts (5 points). Burly smacked this one, and here is the entire deal.

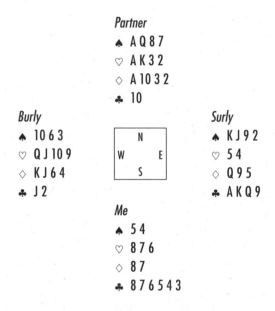

Partner
- ♠ A Q 8 7
- ♡ A K 3 2
- ◇ A 10 3 2
- ♣ 10

Burly
- ♠ 10 6 3
- ♡ Q J 10 9
- ◇ K J 6 4
- ♣ J 2

Surly
- ♠ K J 9 2
- ♡ 5 4
- ◇ Q 9 5
- ♣ A K Q 9

Me
- ♠ 5 4
- ♡ 8 7 6
- ◇ 8 7
- ♣ 8 7 6 5 4 3

Burly followed his double with the sadistic lead of the queen of trumps. When the debris has been cleared away I was down 1100 points. Had I been inspired to pass three clubs, I would have lost only 800 points. Actually I wasn't terribly upset. I had been playing the convention for some time now and was getting used to this kind of result. My partner, however, was a newcomer to the Roman two diamonds, playing it here for the very first time at my insistence. He pointed out in a few thousand well-chosen words that he failed to see any beauty in a convention that required us to play these cards at anything except the level of one.

"Furthermore," he continued, "when you do hold this kind of garbage and hear me open a three-suiter, you just know, if you are any kind of a realist, that the one suit I do not have is clubs — the opponents have the clubs, and if that's the case there is only one bid open to you after I open two diamonds — that bid is pass!"

He was right of course. When you think about it, what other choice is there? It is conceivable that Burly might double, but just barely. More than likely he will think that he has just witnessed another bidding misunderstanding, and if he gives you another chance by opening his mouth you may wake up to the fact that you are playing Roman two-bids and not weak two-bids. After all, his partner only twitched before passing, he did not shake and tremble. So Burly will pass, and your partner will get red in the face and you will go down a measly four hundred points. Not perhaps a great result compared to others, but a certain first among the Romans, and a reaper in my quiz of 25 points.

The second hand arose in a Swiss team game. I was not exactly in love with my opening bid, but I decided that if partner had doubled the overcall for penalties I would have stood for it. After all, my cards, such as they were, seemed defensive in nature. Two spades (10 points) I decided would be a bit cowardly, and a scientific three clubs or three diamonds (5 points) might lead to complications. So I duly doubled (5 points) and these were the four hands:

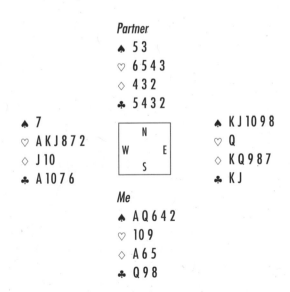

Partner
♠ 5 3
♡ 6 5 4 3
◇ 4 3 2
♣ 5 4 3 2

♠ 7
♡ A K J 8 7 2
◇ J 10
♣ A 10 7 6

♠ K J 10 9 8
♡ Q
◇ K Q 9 8 7
♣ K J

Me
♠ A Q 6 4 2
♡ 10 9
◇ A 6 5
♣ Q 9 8

As you can see, almost any action meant the guillotine. Over my double (5 points) overcaller passed and poor partner decided to shoot it out with a pass. East, who all of a sudden looked more like a tiger than a lamb, redoubled. This time partner removed to two spades and the tigress doubled again. The number was 1400.

To tell you the truth I was not terribly ashamed of what I had done. Certainly I was not sick to the stomach (25 points). "It is quite possible," I said to partner, "that two spades by me would have worked out better. West might just bid her hearts again before her partner had a chance to get at us. Anyway, why worry? They are no doubt playing negative doubles at the other table and the result will be the same."

My partner was not to be mollified. Once again he pointed out that the only conceivable action open to me was pass (25 points). "I know you would have been violating partnership confidence," he said, "but I would forgive you."

Well how did you make out on my quiz? If you were under 30 points then it's back to Culbertson for you. If you managed between 30 and 40 you may tack on Blackwood and Non-forcing Stayman. If you did better than that you don't need any advice from me, for you have proved beyond all doubt, once again, that Bridge is a Solo Sport.

DEAR PARTNER

> *Real-life spouses don't tend to be very good together at the bridge table (although Frank and Lillian Vine were an exception). This is odd when you think about it — it has been said many times that bridge partnerships have a lot in common with marriages. Certainly we hear terms like divorce and remarriage frequently applied in a bridge setting. That being the case, why shouldn't bridge players enter into pre-nuptial agreements?*

You and I are about to embark on that most exciting of life's adventures, a bridge partnership.

Things are not what they used to be. People used to stick together through thick and thin, through win and lose, through triumph and catastrophe. Today it is different. People get divorced at the drop of a trick. There is no level of tolerance. Some blame it on the new morality. I think it is our failure to communicate.

If we simply spelled out at the beginning what it is we expect, then no one would be disappointed when partner turned out to be a little less than another Charles Goren. Take me for instance. My wants are simple. There are only two things I ask of a partner.

One. Be flamboyant with your signals. Here is a typical example.

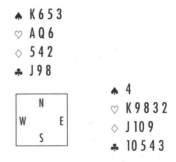

```
              ♠ K 6 5 3
              ♡ A Q 6
              ◇ 5 4 2
              ♣ J 9 8
                          ♠ 4
          ┌─────────┐     ♡ K 9 8 3 2
          │    N    │     ◇ J 10 9
          │ W     E │     ♣ 10 5 4 3
          │    S    │
          └─────────┘
```

South is in four spades with no opposition bidding and the lead is the queen of spades. The declarer wins the king in dummy and then leads a small spade towards his hand. It is your first chance to signal.

Many people will drop the three of clubs. It is against their nature to release an unnecessary high card except at the point of a gun. In effect, they never help on defense.

Then there are those negative inferencers who propose to follow the discard of the small club with that of the nine of diamonds ("It was my smallest diamond, partner."). That shows they want you to lead a heart.

Another group are the high-low Harrys, who pitch the three of hearts. They intend to discard the two of that suit next, thus completing a delicate signal.

The trouble is that there may be no next time. A good declarer will let your partner win the second trick. And what has he seen? A low heart or a low club. The odds are that he is about to go wrong. Sometimes he guesses right, I grant you that. But the wear and tear on his eyes, his nerves, and sometimes his pocketbook, will wear out the partnership.

So bang that big nine of hearts down on the table. Once in a blue moon it may cost a trick. But a million other times it will lead to the best defense, the best result, and a happy partner.

My second rule is, be disrespectful of your betters.

There is a great tendency among players to give their good opponents more than their due. Let them come up against an expert pair, and they freeze. They assume that the stars are always doing something brilliant. Nothing of the sort; they manage as many dumb things as any of us. What makes them experts is that unlike most players they also do a few good things. Here is another hand.

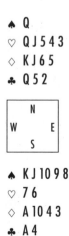

♠ Q
♥ Q J 5 4 3
♦ K J 6 5
♣ Q 5 2

```
        N
    W       E
        S
```

♠ K J 10 9 8
♥ 7 6
♦ A 10 4 3
♣ A 4

By an exotic bidding sequence whose details I am pledged not to reveal, my partner and I arrived at five diamonds. West led the king of hearts, and East's response was to drop the deuce. This was not attitude, and neither was it count; it was baboonery. West obediently shifted to a small club and my queen held. That was a little better. My prospects had improved from three down to two down.

I led the queen of spades. East rose with his ace to return... a club! I won the ace, finessed the jack of diamonds, pulled trumps, and discarded all my losing hearts on the good spades. Making five diamonds.

No Ma'am, it was not a typical hand from the Thursday-night novice game. The event was the Life Master Pairs, and my two opponents are widely considered to be the Garozzo and Belladonna of Canada.

Speaking of Garozzo, I have heard and read about dozens of his brilliancies. But the only time I ever actually sat down against him was for two hands in a National pairs game. On the first hand he doubled us in two spades. My partner made three. On the second Benito was in three notrump, down four.

My conclusion? At any given time during the course of a hand when you are faced with a critical decision based on what your opponents have done, assume that they are a pair of nincompoops. You will be right more often than you will be wrong.

Yours sincerely,
Your partner

HOW I ABOLISHED THE RULE OF RESTRICTED CHOICE

I love Restricted Choice. I love the elegance of the concept, and even more, I love that I can play against people who don't believe in it, which gives me a 2:1 edge. I don't want to spoil the article, so I'll resume editorial comment afterwards rather than continuing now.

I have a new convention. I think, for reasons that will become obvious, it should be named after Sam Fry. I didn't actually invent it, but, as far as I know, no one else has claimed it as his own, and I will be the first to bring it to the attention of the bridge-playing public.

In many ways, it is the most unique convention yet devised. It does not, like Stayman, Blackwood, etc., ask a question, nor does it describe a holding (e.g. the Roman Two Diamonds). What it does do is destroy a mathematical proposition and change the odds in relation to the play of the cards. Sound impossible? Just listen.

It all began on the very first hand of a local game, a small challenge match between two teams. I was playing a contract of four spades and the outcome hinged entirely on the play of the trump suit, all other factors being irrelevant.

Dummy

♠ A K 10 5

[   ]

Declarer

♠ 9 8 7 6 2

I played the ace from the dummy and the queen fell on my right, West producing the three spot. "Aha," I thought, "the rule of restricted choice. I know that one. From a holding of queen-jack doubleton, East will play the queen 50% of the time and the jack 50% of the time. With a singleton queen he will be forced to play it 100% of the time (obviously). Therefore, the odds are two to one in favor of a finesse."

I was about to sail back to my hand to take the hook when my musings were interrupted by a persistent pounding from somewhere on my left.

Annoyed at the turmoil, I swung around and discovered my left-hand opponent was busily hammering on the table.

"Either," I said coldly, "you are trying to disrupt my thinking or you are signalling your partner. In either event, please stop."

"I am trying," he said, equally coldly, "to alert you to a convention." As he spoke, he pointed to his partner's convention card, which I had, of course, neglected to look at before. There it was under Lead Conventions. "We play the queen from all holdings of doubleton queen-jack." As nasty a convention as I had ever seen. The implications of this play were immediately obvious. If my opponent played the queen 100% of the time both from queen-jack and from singleton queen the odds had just shifted from two-to-one back to even money.

"This is insanity," I thought. "No one can change the rules of science with a convention. After all, the rule cannot be a simple question of odds. Somewhere there must be a mathematical formula." I called for paper and pen and swiftly listed the possibilities. There being four cards out in the suit, they would break two-two 40% of the time. These were the possibilities:

3 4	Q J
J 4	Q 3
Q 4	J 3
J 3	Q 4
Q 3	J 4
Q J	3 4

Doubleton queen-jack appears in the East hand just one out of the six times. The percentage of its occurrence is therefore 6.7%. When the suit breaks 3-1 however (50% of the time), the combinations are as follows:

J 4 3	Q
Q 4 3	J
Q J 3	4
Q J 4	3
Q	J 4 3
J	Q 4 3
4	Q J 3
3	Q J 4

The singleton jack or queen each appears in the East hand 6% of the time, and combined appear a total of 12 % of the time, making the mathematical possibility of a singleton honor almost twice that of a doubleton queen-jack. However, the new convention had eliminated a singleton jack from consideration. The queen by itself occurs only 6% of the time. The doubleton queen-jack occurs 6.7% of the time. The latter is therefore slightly more likely. Should the identical situation come up on all 36 boards, my opponent in the next room would finesse 36 times and be right two-thirds of the time. I would finesse and be right only 50% of the time. We would play the same hands in the same manner and yet he would be an easy winner. There just had to be a flaw in my reasoning.

For a moment I thought I had it. Suppose the first play by East was a jack. This would guarantee a singleton — a sure 100% proposition instead of a mere two-to-one shot. Would this not be a great advantage? Not really. My opponent would always take the two-to-one odds anyway and so would be right as often as I was. Then I had a further disturbing thought. "Do you ever," I asked, "psyche the discard and play the jack from a doubleton queen-jack?"

"Only once in a while," was the laconic reply, "when we're looking for a swing."

It was at this black moment that the memory came back to me: Sam Fry and a letter to *The Bridge World*, in which he had questioned the validity of the sacred rule. They had been sneering and derisive. "Get yourself two identical boxes," they said, "and some marbles. And remember to bring lots of money with you."

Well, if they were willing to bet good money on it — I excused myself and left the table, dashing outside to the nearest store. "Give me two identical boxes," I said, "plus three white marbles and one black one."

Assembling my paraphernalia I went to work. Now how did it go? I would place two marbles at random in each box, and then draw one at random from one box. If it proved to be white then the odds were two-to-one that the other marble in that box would also be a white one. The editors of *The Bridge World* made a lot of money betting this way. All at once I felt better. Good old *Bridge World*. They wouldn't risk their money on some hare-brained scheme.

Just to set the record straight, what did the marbles represent? That was easy. One white marble was the queen, one was the jack, and the third was the... ? Well, what was it? The three or the four? And why should it be either one? Surely the correct analogy would be two white marbles and two black marbles. The first two representing the queen and the jack, the other two representing the three and the four. What about the odds then?

If I reached in and picked out a white marble, the odds would be two-to-one that the other marble was black rather than white. Had the four cards consisted of the king, queen, jack and three, then the analogy of the marbles would have been apt. But not in the given situation. "Sam," I thought, "don't bet any more money with those city slickers. They're trying to fleece you."

Quickly back to the playing room where my opponents were beginning to exhibit signs of impatience. What was I to do? All at once a great calm descended upon me. I would fall back on my time-tested method used in all matters of great decision. It was called, "What would Garozzo do?" Well, what would he do? Why it was simple. He would play as he knew the man in the next room would play. This must produce a half on the board. And what would the man in the next room do? Knowing the rule of restricted choice as well as I did, and seeing the queen fall, he would come back to his hand and take the finesse.

Having come to a decision, I played swiftly. Back to my hand, small to the dummy. Small from West, ten from the dummy... the jack from East. Down one! It was like Flint against the Bridge Circus, for 4,000 pounds. It was just as Sam Fry had predicted.

At the post-game party we were congratulating our victorious opponents who had eked out a 3-IMP win. I asked the fellow who sat in my seat in the other room why he had disdained the finesse on hand number one. "Don't you know about the rule of restricted choice?" I inquired.

"Yes, I do," he replied, "but in this case I decided to rely on an older and more hallowed rule."

"Oh," I said, "you mean, with eight ever, nine never?"

"No," he replied, "I mean, one peek is worth two finesses."

In fact, this is exactly why as a defender you are supposed to pick your play randomly from the doubleton QJ — if you give up information the principle of restricted choice goes away, and you are worse off. Basically if you always play the Q from QJ and the J only from singleton J, then you have given up so much information you are hurting yourself.

As declarer playing against the defender who always plays Q from doubleton QJ, when you see the J you should obviously always finesse since the chance of the defender having QJ doubleton is 0%. When you see the Q you should always play for the drop — since the chance of the defender's holding QJ doubleton are 6.78% while the Q alone is 6.22% (about a 9% edge). So you will win 100% of the time if the J appears, and about 55% of the time if the Q shows — odds of almost 3.5 to 1.

If the defenders discard randomly from the doubleton QJ, then declarer, seeing the Q or J fall on his right, has only a little less than 2:1 odds in favor of the finesse: 12.44% (stiff Q or J) versus 6.78% for doubleton QJ.

Your editor is grateful to his son, Colin, for providing this cogent explanation.

LIVE BY THE SWORD... DIE BY THE SWORD

Back when we were publishing our magazine, Canadian Master Point, *Linda and I were very much taken by some articles by Mike Cafferata entitled "Colbert's Rules". We adopted several of Dave Colbert's maxims into our own partnership style; for example, straining to keep the bidding open over partner's 1♣ opening, and not bidding grand slams unless we could count thirteen tricks. But our favorite and most-quoted rule was one that Frank Vine obviously also espoused: Look for reasons to bid, not reasons not to bid. I am embarrassed to admit that the last time I violated it we were actually playing against Dave Colbert, and I lost us 10 IMPs.*

Every player has his golden rule. Some are shrouded in mysticism ("Queens lie over Jacks"), others are a consequence of some old disaster ("Always lead hearts against notrump"). A few are based on practical considerations ("Bid the minor suits, partner. I'll play the notrump"). Let me tell you about my own.

You hold:

♠ A 4 2 ♡ A 4 2 ◇ 7 3 ♣ A Q 8 5 2

Your vulnerable partner opens one diamond and your right hand opponent leaps to four hearts.

The bum!

Well what do you do now? The player who actually held these cards in an IMP match bid four notrump, which he felt was to play, and his partner raised to five diamonds. Well, if four notrump was natural then five diamonds was to play. But suppose he thought four notrump was Blackwood? Deciding to get out before he slid deeper into the pit, our hero passed for a filthy result.

I gave the hand to several other good players. Some bid four notrump, either natural or Blackwood, and a few tried double. In every case the final contract was five diamonds. One intrepid soul plunged into six clubs. This fared a little better since partner held:

♠ 3 ♡ 8 ◇ A K Q 10 9 8 6 ♣ K 9 7 6

Thirteen tricks back to back in diamonds, clubs or notrump. Seven diamonds was the contract at the other table where there was no high level
interference. Is there no way to reach the grand slam after the preempt, or
does the four heart bid make the fix inevitable?

My suggestion (greeted by hoots and shouts of "resulter") was to bid
five hearts. I know, I know. Partner could have loads of hands that would
make slam a disaster. But I also know this. When the opponent draws his
gun it is suicide to run or hide. You have to draw your own gun and shoot
it out. In bridge, there is no other way to survive. Let's look at a couple
more hands.

This time the game is matchpoints. West opens four hearts and partner, vulnerable, passes. You hold:

♠ J 9 5 4 2 ♡ — ◇ K 4 ♣ K J 10 5 3 2

Partner, who passed over four hearts, could easily hold enough cards to
make four spades or five clubs laydown. This time, however, a lot of factors
argue in favor of the pass. Even if game is there in one of your suits, your
action will have to be unilateral and you could well wind up in the wrong
spot. The only way to get both suits in is to make a takeout double and that
action is more likely to bring a five diamond call or a disastrous pass.
Presumably most other players will find themselves in your predicament
and few will take action on their scattered eight-count. To pass is to go with
the field.

Having cleverly thought it all out I passed and the opponents went
down a quiet three undoubled and since partner held

♠ A Q ♡ Q 9 6 3 ◇ A Q 8 7 5 ♣ 9 7

we were cold for game in three suits. Our plus 150 was not quite a bottom
since a few players had failed in slam, but it was close to it. Not because I
was a pussycat and everyone else a mountain lion, but because every other
West had failed to open with a preemptive bid, preferring to start with one
heart, which made our hands easier to handle.

One last hand. Again it's matchpoints. Partner opens one notrump,
strong, and right-hand opponent chirps two clubs, natural. Great! In this

day and age of Cappelletti, Astro, Landy, Brozel and what have you, you are probably the only one in the room faced with this particular problem.

Well, let's figure it out. Your hand is:

♠ A72 ♡ Q532 ◇ 842 ♣ 852

Before the interference you were going to pass and you expected that partner would make his contract, possibly with an overtrick, for a score of 90 or 120. If two clubs is down one, 50, or two, 100 (when you could make 120), then you are getting a bad score. So pass is out. What about two hearts? That's a shot in the dark that will produce a good score only if partner has four hearts. If you are going to put your neck on the chopping block, it might as well be for something worthwhile. The only realistic answer is double. If she makes two clubs you are getting a rotten score doubled or undoubled. But if she goes down...

As it happened I held this hand and doubled, and the declarer went down two. Three hundred was a top and a warning to these opponents never to trifle with us.

Is there a lesson in all this? I think so. When the opponents' bidding is such that any action you take is a total guess, you will guess wrong a reasonable percentage of the time. Therefore take the action that will bring you the highest reward if you guess right. You won't win 'em all, but the opponents will certainly know you've been there.

TEAM MATCH

Bridge is a great leveler — even more than chess, where grand-master Aron Nimzowitsch once stood up at the board in a big tournament and screamed to the heavens, "Why must I lose to this idiot?" Here's Frank Vine's acid retelling of a night where the bridge gods decided to teach the experts a lesson or two.

The pages of *The Kibitzer* are often host to the kind of story best entitled "The Wonder of Me". We are asked to admire the achievements of the writer who is never less than brilliant, even on a bad day. I suppose there are some kinds of klutz who like such articles. All that proves is that there are a lot of klutzes around.

In real life things tend to be a little different. Look at what happened to me last week. My team was playing in a match in the —— IMP league. (Name suppressed to protect the guilty.) It is a wildly unbalanced league. There are a few experienced teams, like mine. The rest range from mediocre to god-awful. My team is certainly the class of the league. North, my partner, has a lot of wins to his credit, and our teammates are polished veterans. Our opponents this night? The bottom of the barrel. For us to sully our hands and play them was almost a joke. Here is how the joke went.

East-West vulnerable
Dealer West

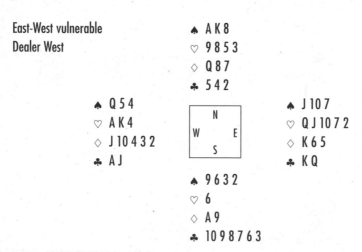

```
                    ♠ A K 8
                    ♡ 9 8 5 3
                    ◇ Q 8 7
                    ♣ 5 4 2
    ♠ Q 5 4                          ♠ J 10 7
    ♡ A K 4            N             ♡ Q J 10 7 2
    ◇ J 10 4 3 2   W      E          ◇ K 6 5
    ♣ A J             S              ♣ K Q
                    ♠ 9 6 3 2
                    ♡ 6
                    ◇ A 9
                    ♣ 10 9 8 7 6 3
```

West bid a notrump and East transferred with 2◊. At least, their card claimed they were playing Jacoby transfers. But West neither alerted nor bid and 2◊ became the final contract. East was in a rage.

"We're cold for 4♡," he snarled. "Can't you remember anything?"

My partner kindly pointed out that four hearts was down one (two spades and two diamonds). And that is exactly what happened at the other table. Four hearts down one, and doubled! Our opponents' dumb mistake hadn't cost them a nickel. I wonder what I would have felt like had I known this was to be our luckiest result.

Again they used a transfer auction.

Both vulnerable
Dealer East

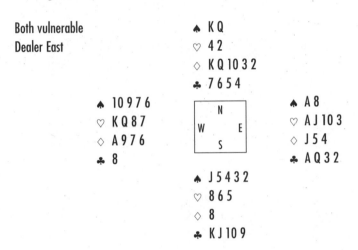

♠ K Q
♡ 4 2
◊ K Q 10 3 2
♣ 7 6 5 4

♠ 10 9 7 6
♡ K Q 8 7
◊ A 9 7 6
♣ 8

♠ A 8
♡ A J 10 3
◊ J 5 4
♣ A Q 3 2

♠ J 5 4 3 2
♡ 8 6 5
◊ 8
♣ K J 10 9

This time East started the notrump. West remembered about transfers but forgot how they worked. He bid 2♡, thinking he was giving partner a choice of suits. Partner obediently bid 2♠, and West raised to 3♠ — invitational, as he later explained.

I have a theory about opening leads in this kind of situation. When you are long in trumps, it pays to lead your long outside suit (here, clubs). It's called "establishing the pump". (Listen to me; you might learn something.) This time it was the only lead to let the contract make. East cashed two clubs (pitching a heart from dummy), ruffed a club, came to his hand with a heart, ruffed his last club, cashed his second heart and the ace of diamonds, and tried to cash a third heart. Partner ruffed and fired back his trump. But declarer produced the fourth heart making his ten of trumps *en passant*. That was 140 for the bad guys.

At the other table partners played in the inferior contract of 4♡. On a trump lead this was held to nine tricks. So much for the over-publicized four-four fit.

After that we bid a great slam, then a dumb one, then a good game, then a dumb one, and at the end of the half we were in front by one miserable IMP.

The rest of the room was chuckling. Chuckling? They were convulsed. We sat down for the second half grimly determined. There would be no more fooling around. This was going to be a bloodbath.

This was deal one of the massacre.

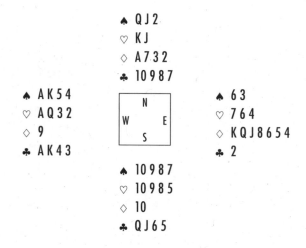

```
                    ♠ Q J 2
                    ♡ K J
                    ◇ A 7 3 2
                    ♣ 10 9 8 7
    ♠ A K 5 4          ┌───────┐        ♠ 6 3
    ♡ A Q 3 2          │   N   │        ♡ 7 6 4
    ◇ 9            W   │       │   E    ◇ K Q J 8 6 5 4
    ♣ A K 4 3          │   S   │        ♣ 2
                       └───────┘
                    ♠ 10 9 8 7
                    ♡ 10 9 8 5
                    ◇ 10
                    ♣ Q J 6 5
```

Partner, an aggressive bidder, familiar with the principle of taking full advantage of the vulnerability, opened the North hand with one diamond. After two passes West, a novice, tried an old-fashioned two diamonds; strong, artificial, and forcing to game. East, who had never heard of what happens to people who breach discipline, passed. They made four. Well, at least West hadn't reopened with a double. We might still be bleeding.

At the other table North, an unimaginative clod, checked his shortage of aces and kings and points and passed. West got to open with one club, heard a diamond response from his partner, and with his twenty gilt-edged points was never willing to settle under game. Three notrump seemed right, but that was 300 in the soup. The dummies had struck again.

This wasn't funny any more. On the next deal it got downright tragic.

North-South vulnerable
Dealer East

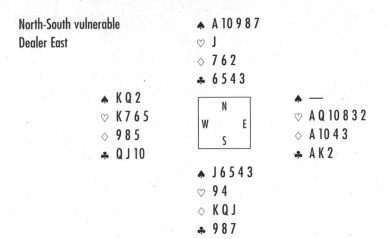

```
                      ♠ A 10 9 8 7
                      ♡ J
                      ◇ 7 6 2
                      ♣ 6 5 4 3
    ♠ K Q 2                            ♠ —
    ♡ K 7 6 5          N               ♡ A Q 10 8 3 2
    ◇ 9 8 5        W       E           ◇ A 10 4 3
    ♣ Q J 10           S               ♣ A K 2
                      ♠ J 6 5 4 3
                      ♡ 9 4
                      ◇ K Q J
                      ♣ 9 8 7
```

When our partners were East-West, the dealer started with 1♡, got a limit raise to three and went straight to six. No information to the enemy. South didn't need information. He led a diamond and that was down one.

At our table East started with 2♣. A terrible bid, in my opinion. West said 2♡, another terrible bid, and opener went straight to six.

Partner did just what I would have done. He led his ♠A. I have a theory about leading against slams. (Another free lesson for you.) If you have an ace, lead it. It will work a hundred times out of a hundred. This was the hundred and first time. East ruffed, pulled trump, and ditched two diamonds on two good spades. Making 6♡.

You would think that this was enough. But Fate had one more low blow in store.

```
    ♠ Q J 9                        ♠ A 10 6 5
    ♡ A K            N              ♡ 4
    ◇ 7 6 5      W        E         ◇ A K J 10 9 8
    ♣ K 10 5 4 3      S             ♣ A 2
```

Our partners reached this lovely little diamond slam. East began things with 1◇ and, after that, was able to diagnose the perfect mesh of cards. I make the slam about 80%. It needs diamonds to behave; failing that, clubs three-three; and failing that, the spade finesse has to work. South held three diamonds to the queen and the king of spades, and clubs were four-two. Unlucky!

At our table East started with one spade. Apparently he had just invented canapé. West tried two clubs, East rebid two mighty diamonds, and when West leaped to 3 NT, he passed. Game, set and match.

The moral of all this? Not that anyone can beat you on a given day. We all know that. But that the line between good and bad is a thin one, and the player who underestimates his opponents because of past performance is very apt to wind up with a lot of egg on his face.

THE HUDDLERS STRIKE BACK

Most of the readers of this book will be too young to remember Stephen Potter's humorous classic, which gave us the word gamesmanship. Bridge is a game where circumstances demand high ethical standards be maintained, else it were impossible to play at all. And where those standards are not maintained, it is but a short step before we have situations where the "c" word is being bandied about. We have all played against Wendell Weasel and his wife, and come away the worse for the experience. In this article, Vine unerringly skewers the hesitators — and, as you laugh at it, you may find yourself realizing that it really isn't very humorous at all.

Fellow Huddlers. It is hard to believe that less than two short years have passed since that black October day the bridge establishment, not content with their superiority in bidding, play and partnership, attacked the last bastion of the underprivileged, and cold-bloodedly banned the huddle.

Do I need to remind you how good it used to be? An opponent opened the bidding. Partner, with any kind of questionable call, simply pondered over the hand for a lengthy period of time and passed. It was easy then to take the right action. Oh, there was a sort of rule that was supposed to interfere with us, but it was so hard to interpret that generally we got away with anything short of hijacking. Then came the new wording. If partner huddled you could only take the action that 80% of your peers would take with your hand had there been no hesitation. With one foul blow the bidding structure was shattered. Then, as so often happens, action bred a reaction.

It began with the brilliant coup originated by our former honored member from Kapuskasing, Wendell Weasel, in partnership with his good wife Wendy. This was the hand.

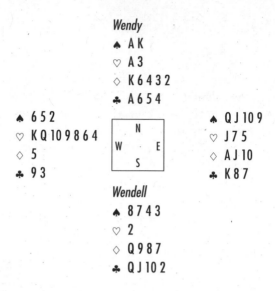

Wendy
♠ A K
♡ A 3
◇ K 6 4 3 2
♣ A 6 5 4

♠ 6 5 2
♡ K Q 10 9 8 6 4
◇ 5
♣ 9 3

♠ Q J 10 9
♡ J 7 5
◇ A J 10
♣ K 8 7

Wendell
♠ 8 7 4 3
♡ 2
◇ Q 9 8 7
♣ Q J 10 2

West was the dealer and opened three hearts. Wendy Weasel faced a nasty problem. There are lots of points but no tricks. A double might bring spades, and three notrump might bring a double. Both would be unwelcome. She gave the matter long consideration and finally passed. East also passed and Wendell boldly entered the auction with a double. Mrs. Weasel did not hang her nice balancing partner for keeping the bidding open; she made the intelligent minimum call of four diamonds, which became the final contract. When dummy came down the shriek for the director was heard from the Bay of Fundy to Vancouver Island.

"What happened?" he asked.

West, a sneerer, told his version. "I opened with three hearts," he said. "This lady goes into a trance for an hour and passes, and her partner says 'double'. Just take a look at that pile of junk. Do you call that a legitimate double?"

He spoke with that tone of outraged virtue common to those who know the establishment is bound to protect them. The director turned to Wendell.

"Are those facts substantially correct, sir?" he asked.

"No," said Wendell, "they are not. My partner did not hesitate in any way, shape or form."

While East and West foamed at the mouth, the director remained unruffled.

"Let me put it like this," he said. "West opened three hearts and your partner had a problem."

"No," said Weasel, "she had no problem at all. She passed like a flash. Ask her yourself."

Wendy was quick to agree with her husband. "I didn't hesitate at all," she said. "I passed right away."

Well, sir. You should have heard the hooting and the hollering and the stomping, all to no avail, of course. If one pair says it didn't huddle and the other pair says it did, the director is helpless. He did, however, make one more try.

"Do you generally come in with hands like that in balancing seat?" he inquired.

"No one steals from me," said Wendell Weasel.

The Weasel solution, to deny that huddle even occurred, was simple, brilliant and effective. Do not, however, make the mistake of its founder who fell in love with his invention and tried to use it three more times that same afternoon. His being barred for twenty years from the ACBL should be a lesson to all of us on the merits of moderation.

Now I would like to discuss with you a few of the newer conventions.

One of the more vexing problems in bridge is how to show a void when partner asks for aces. Some jump around with one ace and a void, others with two aces and a void, and a few cunning souls lie by two aces and then bid the void suit later. All methods work in some instances and cause headaches in others. My solution is to use Keycard Huddle Blackwood. It goes like this.

Partner bids four notrump and you have a void. Just pause for a significant moment and then bid your correct number of aces. Since there is never any cause to think when your partner uses Blackwood, the huddle must be clearcut. You have a certified void.

How do you explain your hesitation to an inquisitive director or a nosy opponent? Just tell them you didn't know whether your partner's four notrump was quantitative or qualitative and that it took you a bit of time to decide. This statement always seems to impress the better type of director. If he asks how you show voids, just say that you never do. You simply rely on partner's table presence.

Another convention I have found useful is fumble leads. One of the great debates has centered around the lead from three small in an unbid suit. One school holds out firmly for the top of nothing, claiming that the quality of the holding is what partner is primarily interested in. Others advocate leading small from three, saying that the count is of first importance. Then there are MUD and Journalist leads. Both have their ups and downs. The former because it often delivers its message too late; and as for the latter... lives there a Journalist leader about to produce the unreadable lead of the eight from K-J-8-2 who doesn't feel in his bones that he and his partner are about to cooperate in yet another classic debacle?

The answer to all this is fumble leads. It works like this. You hold 8-6-3 in a suit and lead the eight. Partner cashes the king and produces the ace. On the play to this trick you balk just the tiniest bit before playing the six. Your delicate hesitation has now clarified the matter for your partner. No false-carding opponent can ever deceive him as to the location of the three. It just has to be nestling snugly in your hand, and he can take the appropriate action.

Finally for the scientific, control-showing huddles, a convention based on the Italian Neapolitan system. As you know, in the Blue Team Club, the answer to a forcing club shows not suits, not points, but controls, with a king counted as one control and an ace as two. We have adapted this system to skip-bid situations.

Your opponent announces a skip bid and opens three diamonds. Most of us are familiar with the normal huddles in use today. A loud count to ten, a jocular look at your watch, or an obvious lack of interest in the proceedings indicates a bad hand. An intense study of the cards throughout the ten-second period, followed by a further wait, followed by a sad pass, shows a hand not able to take immediate action (without risk) but, nevertheless, a hand with possibilities.

Although all this is generally effective and widely adopted, I think that better use can be made of this pause. A fast pass (i.e., after counting loudly to ten) shows two controls or fewer. A long study of the hand followed by a mournful pass shows three to four controls. Anything more shows better than four controls. One advantage of all this is that when partner reopens there is never any reason to jump the bidding. Having already shown your controls, you simply bid your long suit. Here is a hand on which partner and I achieved an outstanding result.

Partner

♠ K Q 2
♡ Q 10 4
◇ 6 5
♣ A K Q 8 3

[   ]

Me

♠ A J 10 9 8
♡ A K J 8 7
◇ 4 3
♣ 7

My left-hand opponent opened three diamonds and my partner gave it the long pause showing three or four controls. This could be at most A-K of clubs and king of spades. When I doubled, he bid four clubs showing his suit and I settled in four hearts. You'd be surprised how many people got into trouble on this hand.

One more thing. In evaluating their controls, many players prefer to place the king of the preempted suit in a special category. They feel it is a good card if the destination is notrump but generally useless if you wind up someplace else. For the purposes of the huddle they do not count the king as a control. If partner reopens with a double they then bid three notrump. This is called "The Impossible Negative Huddle" and always specifically shows the king of the preemptor's suit.

There are more of these conventions available, but I am running out of space and energy. Study those I have put before you and give them an honest try. That's all I ask. Maybe you too will prove once again that he who hesitates is not necessarily lost.

THOSE WERE THE DAYS, MY FRIEND

> *In the Introduction to his book* The Hands of Time, BRIDGE *Magazine editor Mark Horton addresses this same question: is the play of today's experts better than that of the players who have participated in the great Championships down the years? He quoted Edgar Kaplan, who said, "I doubt that today's best players are the equal of the best of the past. Today's partnerships are clearly better. Today's youth are interested in bidding, not card play… [but] the card players of old were usually a trick or two too high. The best then were more creative than today." Horton agrees, concluding that while there are more strong players now than in 1950, and many of them are perhaps more technically proficient, the individual expert may not in the final analysis have attained a clearly higher level.*
>
> *But you don't have to take his word for it. Read on, and try Frank's quiz…*

In a most provocative article ("Challenge Yesterday's Champs," *The Bridge World*, February 1983), the authors, Maurice LaRochelle and Eric Kokish, make the blunt submission that modem bridge experts clearly rank a cut over those of the past. Newer is better. That's the gospel of today, and everyone (everyone who is anyone) is asked to agree. Well, not me. I think that's a bunch of hogwash.

Oh, we do improve, I'll concede that much. Better food, better training, better steroids have seen to that. Men run faster, and teenage girls swim like fish. But in matters of the mind, and bridge is a matter of the mind, the trend is in the other direction.

Consider this. When did you last whistle a tune that would make George Gershwin sit up and take notice? And what new play have you been to that belongs in the same world as Eugene O'Neill? And when did you last read a book that lives in the heart, or thrill to the beauty of music, or cry at a movie? Not unless they were written a long time ago. I'll bet you on that.

It's the same with bridge. Bidding may be more useful, but in play, defense or sleight of hand, I can't see that today's player has any kind of edge. That's only opinion, of course. LaRochelle and Kokish seem to have other ideas. So, I, too, have designed a quiz. In each case you have only one major question to answer. Are we talking old (pre-1965) or are we talking new (post-1970)? I have skipped the intervening five years to create a clearer division.

To make it easier, I have slipped in a few clues. Some of those, however, are designed to lead you astray, just as in a good mystery novel (and when did you last read one of those?). Okay. Let's start!

1. You are South, holding:

♠ A K 9 6   ♡ 8 6   ◇ 10 8 4   ♣ A 4 3 2

The bidding goes like this:

WEST	NORTH	EAST	SOUTH
	pass	pass	1♠
dbl	4♠	pass	pass
5♡	5♠	pass	pass
6♡	pass	pass	6♠
7♡	pass	pass	7♠
dbl	all pass		

Well! Has everyone at the table gone berserk, or is there method in this madness? And, what do you think, are we talking old or are we talking new? This may help. Why didn't South open the bidding one club? Is he an old-fashioned four-card-majorite? Or is he perhaps playing a strong-club system like Neapolitan?

2.
South dealer
East-West vulnerable

Dummy

♠ A K 7
♡ K 8 5 4
◇ Q 10 2
♣ J 10 9

♠ J 9 8 3
♡ J 3
◇ K J 3
♣ A 6 5 4

```
      N
  W       E
      S
```

There are two passes to North, who opens one heart; East passes; one notrump by South; double by West; all pass. You, West, lead a small spade: king from dummy, small from the others. Declarer now plays two rounds of clubs. Your partner follows, showing a doubleton, and you duck. Now declarer plays the third club, overtaking it in his hand. Defend!

Oh, yes, your clue. If you do well in this event, you will win the McKenney Trophy for the year. That's not too surprising. If they had a vote for the best matchpoint player of all time, you would win in a breeze.

3.
        Dummy

        ♠ 8 6
        ♡ 7 4
        ◇ A K 9 7 6 4
        ♣ 10 7 6

♠ 10 7 4 3
♡ 9 5 2
◇ Q 10 5
♣ K 9 5

```
      N
   W     E
      S
```

Once again you are West, on opening lead, this time against six notrump. It's matchpoints, and South has described a powerful balanced hand, 23 or 24 points. You lead a heart. Declarer wins partner's ten with the jack, travels to the king of diamonds in dummy (partner follows with the deuce), leads a small spade from dummy, and puts in the queen. On the reasonable assumption that you may be getting in with a diamond, how do you plan your defense? Just one hint here: the contract went down two!

4.
        ♠ 9 4 3
        ♡ A K 4
        ◇ A 4
        ♣ A 10 9 8 6

```
      N
   W     E
      S
```

        ♠ A K Q J 8 7 6
        ♡ 8 3
        ◇ 5
        ♣ J 4 3

WEST	NORTH	EAST	SOUTH
	1♣	1♡	4♠
pass	6♠	all pass	

The lead is the two of hearts; you win in dummy with the king. It looks like a classic strip, so you lead a trump — but East shows out. Well, there goes that dream. What now? Will you try the best technical line, or is this perhaps the time for a deceptive move? One word of caution: your opponents are not Americans; notwithstanding that, they are both good players. One, in fact, has a claim to the title "best in the world". So how do you play?

Answers

1.

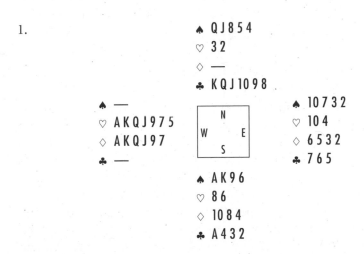

```
            ♠ Q J 8 5 4
            ♡ 3 2
            ◇ —
            ♣ K Q J 10 9 8
♠ —                           ♠ 10 7 3 2
♡ A K Q J 9 7 5   N           ♡ 10 4
◇ A K Q J 9 7   W   E         ◇ 6 5 3 2
♣ —               S           ♣ 7 6 5
            ♠ A K 9 6
            ♡ 8 6
            ◇ 10 8 4
            ♣ A 4 3 2
```

The bidding on this deal was both inspired and delicate. It was perhaps one of the best-bid deals in the history of bridge. West, certain of a grand slam in two suits, certain, too, that his opponents must have a cheap sacrifice, with nerves of steel went just one level higher at every turn. Unluckily for him, South was Mr. "You have to be at the table," Oswald Jacoby himself. And he diagnosed the maneuver. When seven hearts came round to him he decided it was being bid to make. That could mean only one thing. Thirteen red cards. How do I know what he thought? Just look at how he played the hand.

The opening lead was the ace of diamonds. Jacoby ruffed with the eight of spades, led the four of trumps from dummy, and, when East played low, put in the six! Now, a ruff of a diamond with the jack of spades, a trump to his nine, and a diamond ruffed by the queen. Finally, a club to the ace — and claim. When did all this happen? More than thirty years ago.

2.

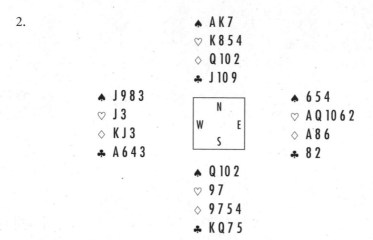

```
                        ♠ A K 7
                        ♡ K 8 5 4
                        ◇ Q 10 2
                        ♣ J 10 9
        ♠ J 9 8 3                         ♠ 6 5 4
        ♡ J 3              N              ♡ A Q 10 6 2
        ◇ K J 3        W       E          ◇ A 8 6
        ♣ A 6 4 3          S              ♣ 8 2
                        ♠ Q 10 2
                        ♡ 9 7
                        ◇ 9 7 5 4
                        ♣ K Q 7 5
```

Did you win the third club, and switch? Good! You score 100, and earn your usual average.

The real West was Barry Crane (I'll bet you guessed that). And Crane was not one to play for average. When the declarer led the third club from dummy and overtook in his hand, Crane ducked again! With four tricks home, and two more guaranteed, the declarer decided to go for it; he led a small diamond to the ten and ace. Another spade came back. This time, declarer fell from grace. He won in his hand, to lead a second diamond.

Crane drove home the bayonet. He rose with the king, and now, at last, played his ace of clubs. Dummy was squeezed. Eventually, declarer threw a heart; Crane's lead of the jack of hearts sealed his doom. Plus 300 meant all the marbles, and Barry Crane had won his first McKenney trophy. The year? 1952.

3.

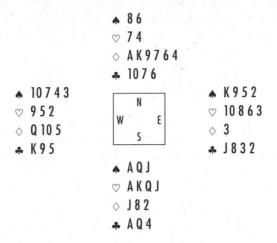

♠ 8 6
♥ 7 4
♦ A K 9 7 6 4
♣ 10 7 6

♠ 10 7 4 3
♥ 9 5 2
♦ Q 10 5
♣ K 9 5

♠ K 9 5 2
♥ 10 8 6 3
♦ 3
♣ J 8 3 2

♠ A Q J
♥ A K Q J
♦ J 8 2
♣ A Q 4

Did you ever hear of Harry Merkle? Not unless you've seen this deal before. Yet Harry was one of the fine players who traveled the California Circuit around 1947, when this deal arose. The declarer, in six notrump, convinced Merkle by the early play that the contract was on ice. So Harry decided to make him an offer he couldn't refuse. When declarer, after winning the spade finesse, impeccably led the jack of diamonds, Merkle played the ten!

Now, there are a few players around (from Mars, all of them) who would still play low from dummy. But, being human, and playing matchpoints, this declarer went up with the ace, cashed the king — and lost the whole diamond suit. Down two! As Merkle put it, the par result.

4.

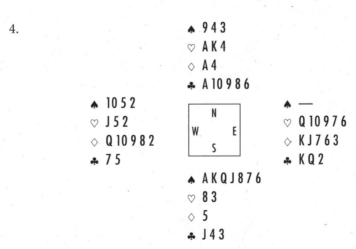

♠ 9 4 3
♥ A K 4
♦ A 4
♣ A 10 9 8 6

♠ 10 5 2
♥ J 5 2
♦ Q 10 9 8 2
♣ 7 5

♠ —
♥ Q 10 9 7 6
♦ K J 7 6 3
♣ K Q 2

♠ A K Q J 8 7 6
♥ 8 3
♦ 5
♣ J 4 3

The game was rubber bridge. The place, London. Sitting West, Leslie Dodds. Sitting East, Terence Reese. Not the kind of opponents you would search out, unless you had a lot of money to spend.

South was a pretty fair country player himself. His name, John Crawford. In those days, around 1950, there were a lot of people who considered him the toughest man who ever sat down at the table.

Crawford won the heart lead, and tested the spades. When Reese showed out, it looked as though declarer must fall back on the double finesse in clubs, a reasonable chance. But Crawford felt that Reese might well hold both club honors, in view of his overcall. He decided to play on the assumption that Reese held exactly five hearts (because of the lead), and at least three clubs. On that basis, he led out four more rounds of trumps, a total of five. Reese could not afford to throw a club; he had to come down to four red cards, as did dummy.

Crawford watched the discards closely. When Reese bared down to three hearts and a diamond, Crawford played the ace of diamonds and ruffed a diamond. Reese was forced to disgorge another heart; now came ace of hearts, heart ruff. Then jack of clubs. Endplay!

Reese later called it one of the best hands he had ever seen played at the table. Personally I never argue with Terence Reese.

As you can see, the whole thing has been a fraud. There are no deals from the present. However, can you look at these hands and swallow the LaRochelle-Kokish dictum about today's stars? If you're still not convinced, read the report on the last world championship, and take a hard look at all the idiocies. If that doesn't convince you, you're hopeless.

TWO BRIDGE TALES

Golf has its nineteenth hole, and every bridge club has some nearby restaurant or watering hole where the players can repair after the game to rehash the hands and tell stories. Here are two of Frank's favorites. I can't personally vouch for the first, but from my own knowledge of the Moo Cow, it would be typical of him. The second story I know to be gospel. I heard it some years ago directly from "Mr. Fuddle", who is a close personal friend; he had not realized until our research unearthed this piece that the incident had been recounted by Frank in the Kibitzer. I also know the identity of "Mr. Duddle", but the laws of libel and my hopes of a financially secure retirement both strongly suggest maintaining confidentiality.

So little has been written of the history of bridge that many of its golden moments have gone unreported. Here are two of them.

The time: the swinging sixties. The place: Toronto's Royal York Hotel, the Easter Regional. The occasion: the presentation of the Micky Miller Trophy, awarded to the player winning the most masterpoints during the year.

The scenario was always the same. During the second half of the Open Pairs the play was halted. The president of the Unit announced the winner (polite applause). The winner stood up to speak (groans), he admitted he had been lucky (more polite applause). He confided that he really was unworthy of the honor. (Hear! Hear!) Then it was all back to the game. Basically it was a bore.

This time, however, the feeling was different, for the winner of the Miller Trophy was no one else than that master of the rough tongue, Don "the Moo Cow" Cowan. Whatever he had to say it was not apt to be the traditional humble mumble. The betting was that he would leave at least a dozen people frothing at the mouth in anger.

It was, however, a different Cowan who stood up to speak. His voice was low and controlled. There was a sincerity and emotionalism there that none of us had ever heard before.

"Last year," he began, "the winner of the Miller Trophy was Sami Kehela. He stood on this very spot and spoke these words, 'You don't win the Miller Trophy unless you have good partners.'"

Cowan paused for a moment to sip some water. Then he continued, "Well, I proved he was wrong!"

Well, sir, you should have heard the cheers.

My second story is about two well-known Canadian players whom I will refer to only as Fuddle and Duddle. Fuddle was the quiet one. He never raised his voice or his tone. He was the rarest of the bridge breed, a non-criticizer. Duddle was the opposite. Volatile and quick-tempered, you could always count on him to castigate his partner whenever he thought things had been done badly. Eventually Fuddle got tired of the abuse and broke up the partnership.

Two months went by and Fuddle received a telephone call. "This is Duddle," said the caller. "I have had a lot of time to think things over and I decided you were entirely right. My behavior was unforgivable. I think I have learned my lesson and I would like very much to play with you again. Tomorrow there is a Regional Men's Pairs in Ottawa and I was hoping you would play with me."

Well, Fuddle was reluctant. He knew that a bridge leopard is hardly likely to change his spots, but finally he allowed himself to be persuaded. As he lived in Toronto he had to get up very early the next day to make the long drive to Ottawa. Since the weather was dirty and the roads were winding, the trip was a nasty one and it was only with moments to spare that he entered the playing hall, threw his coat on a chair, said "Hello" to Duddle and sat down to play.

The first board was a dandy. One of those hands where all bid like mad because no one knows who can make what. Finally Duddle bid four spades, the opponents intervened with five hearts and Fuddle was faced with the classic decision. To double or bid one more. Finally he decided to take out insurance and raised to five spades. "Double!" said the enemy and the opening lead was made and Fuddle faced his cards.

As Duddle examined the dummy a slow wave of red rose from his chest to his forehead and he rose part way out of his seat to snarl, "You moron!"

There was a moment's silence, and then in a calm, contained voice Fuddle said, "You know something, you're absolutely right," and he stood up, put on his coat and drove back to Toronto.

The moral? Gibraltar may tumble, the Rockies may crumble, but a bridge player is here to stay.

SO LONG, DAD

*I didn't know Bill Milligan, but after reading this bridge obitu-
ary, I feel as though I did. And I think I'm glad I never played
against him. For those of you puzzled by Dad's lead-director on
the first deal, think* Maltese Falcon...

Bill Milligan is dead.

To most of you that won't mean a thing. To a few of us it's the end of
an era. A time to hoist a tankard or two and toast a legend. Because his
game was usually rubber bridge, his exploits have never been recorded. Bill
Milligan (or "Dad", as he was known to his cronies) was not a great player.
He was certainly the biggest crook the game has ever seen.

Now when I say "crook", I don't mean cheat. Touching toes under the
table, scribbling down false scores, wiring leads — all those were, for
Milligan, beneath contempt. Dad had style. Even the most bloodied of his
victims were apt to join in the applause. For instance:

Toronto 1970
Regional Mixed Pairs

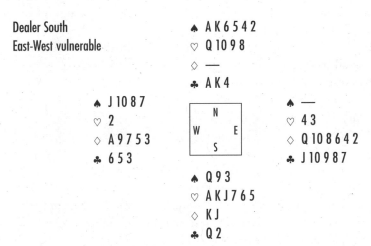

Dealer South
East-West vulnerable

♠ A K 6 5 4 2
♡ Q 10 9 8
◇ —
♣ A K 4

♠ J 10 8 7   ♠ —
♡ 2   ♡ 4 3
◇ A 9 7 5 3   ◇ Q 10 8 6 4 2
♣ 6 5 3   ♣ J 10 9 8 7

♠ Q 9 3
♡ A K J 7 6 5
◇ K J
♣ Q 2

South opened 1♡, West passed, and invariably North bid 5NT. What
should East do? Most players waited until their opponents reached 7♡, and
then tried a Lightner double. Alas, partner proved unimaginative and led

the ◊ A. A few adventurers bid a lead-directing 6♠ over 5NT and took their lumps in 7◊ doubled. Dad, who put little faith in conventions and none in the astuteness of partners, found a different solution.

"It's your lead, Sam," he said.

Milligan was famous for his powers of observation. Big and burly as he was, his size wedded to an agile neck, it was a rare opponent who was able to keep his cards hidden from those roving eyes. I remember this hand from a rubber game.

Dad	Dummy
♠ A 9 8 5 4	♠ Q 10 8 6
♡ 6 4	♡ A K
◊ 5 3 2	◊ A K Q
♣ 5 4 3	♣ A K Q J

Dad was declarer in 7♠. He had already taken his view and spotted the king and one trump in RHO's hand. What to do? Dad called to a kibitzer.

"Would you mind going to the shelf and getting a copy of Goren, and looking this up? What does he say you play when you're missing king and one in a suit? Do you hook or play for the drop?"

Indignant opponents would not allow the inquiry to go any further, but when Dad led the ♠Q from dummy, East ducked smoothly.

When a committee was convened, Dad blamed it all on his opponents. "The nerve of that guy," he said. "Eavesdropping."

He was also a student of bidding philosophy. Witness his solution to defining a good six-card suit in a hand just under a game force — a problem that has vexed theoreticians from Vanderbilt to C. C. Wei.

"Acol Charlie bids two hearts," he announced.

This story, however, concerns a side of Milligan that few know about. It reveals a man conscious of the traditions of the game and a defender of its values.

The tournament was being held in Toronto. Dad and I had been having a reasonable game, and as the event was drawing to a close, we approached a table surrounded by a mountain of kibitzers. In Toronto this meant only one thing. We were about to face Murray and Kehela.

This was the second board. My hand:

♠ 6 4 2   ♡ A J 7 6 5   ◊ 4 3 2   ♣ K 5

The bidding was short. Dad opened 2NT and I raised to three. Eric Murray led the ♠K.

It went small, large, the ace from Milligan. Then the two of clubs from Dad, the three from Murray, the five from dummy, and… the four from Kehela!

Well sir, you should have been there.

Murray's cigar dropped on the table. Kehela's followed. A wave of sound swept the army of kibitzers. One woman in the seventh row kept yelling, "I can't see! What did he do? What did he do?"

Another voice replied, "He finessed the five, by God, he finessed the five!"

I sat enthralled. Partner had daringly created an extra entry to dummy. How would he use it?

The crowd hushed and tensed as he pondered. One minute went by, two, five. Finally he made his move.

"Play the king of clubs."

In a daze I obeyed. Kehela showed out and Dad overtook with his ace. This was how the cards lay.

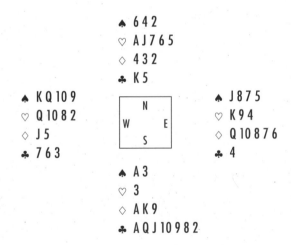

We left the table enveloped in an eerie silence. One of the kibitzers followed.

"Are you crazy, Dad?" he asked. "Taking a finesse like that for no reason. You must have seen Murray's hand."

"No one sees Murray's cards," said Dad. "He's an expert," and stalked off.

The kibitzer was puzzled. "What's he mad about?"

"Boy, are you dumb," I replied. "Let some dumbo finesse a queen to gain a trick and he's bright. Let a person finesse a five-spot for no gain and he's a cretin. What does bridge mean to you, anyway? One more master-point? A way to earn money?

"Well, let me tell you something. To Dad a great play is a great play whether you win or lose, or even when there is nothing to win at all.

"Dad might have needed that entry to dummy and Murray's correct play was to split his clubs. But because it was Milligan playing the hand and not Forquet, Murray gave it no thought and carelessly played low. That was a mistake and Dad pointed it out by finessing the five.

"'Mr. Expert,' he was saying, 'when I play the hand I want you to pay attention. If you don't, you may get your fingers burned.' The dogmeat had talked back to the top dog, not with words but through the language of card play."

I caught up to my partner.

"That was a nice play, Dad," I said.

"It was the *only* play," said Milligan.

Parody

YOU BE THE JUDGE (AS IT SHOULD BE)

"You Be the Judge" was a popular feature of The Bridge World *in the 1970s. Basically a deal was presented that featured a disaster in bidding and play, and the members of an expert panel were asked to assign the blame. The appeal was similar to that of being able to watch investigators piece together an aircraft after a fatal crash...*

You have asked for constructive criticism of the features in your magazine. May I suggest that "You Be the Judge" could stand improvement. For one thing, I would like to see a full background for each hand. It increases the empathy. Another fault lies in your choice of panel. Why pick a group of bridge players? Is there anyone less likely to come to an impartial decision? If you are going to judge something you use people skilled in tackling problems; or, better yet, you use real judges. Let me give you an example or two.

Problem Number One arose in a recent pairs event and involved that well-known Canadian pair, Boswell Blabbermouth and his wife, Alice. They were, as you doubtless have heard, an inspiration to us all. Alice bid only the minor suits, always returned her husband's lead, and never excused her occasional mistakes on the grounds that the housework was getting her down, the baby's colic was keeping her up, or that her husband had been gazing too admiringly at that blonde at the next table. For his part, Boswell rarely snapped or snarled and was quick to compliment his wife on the excellence of her finessing, which was the best part of her game. Then along came this hand.

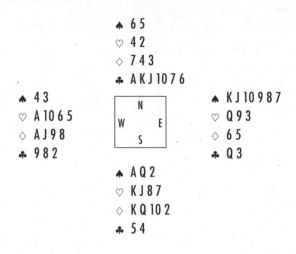

```
                    ♠ 6 5
                    ♡ 4 2
                    ◇ 7 4 3
                    ♣ A K J 10 7 6
    ♠ 4 3                          ♠ K J 10 9 8 7
    ♡ A 10 6 5        N            ♡ Q 9 3
    ◇ A J 9 8      W     E         ◇ 6 5
    ♣ 9 8 2           S            ♣ Q 3
                    ♠ A Q 2
                    ♡ K J 8 7
                    ◇ K Q 10 2
                    ♣ 5 4
```

WEST	NORTH	EAST	SOUTH
Boswell		*Alice*	
		2♠	2NT
pass	3NT	all pass	

Boswell dutifully led his highest spade. Declarer topped the jack with his queen and led the five of clubs. It went two, ten, *three*!

After this remarkable duck by Alice, the contract is doomed. The declarer leads a diamond to his hand, Boswell wins this with the ace and fires back a spade, dislodging the last stopper. Now comes a repeat of the "successful" club finesse and Alice wins the queen to run her good spades. The unbreakable contract is broken. Only something happened.

No sooner had the first club play been completed than Blabbermouth turned to the declarer and confided, "So you've got that card too."

Now the declarer may not have been what the Italians like to call "The Raphael of the Bridge Table", but neither was he a Denny Dimwit. He banged down the ace and the rest of the clubs and made his contract with an overtrick.

Alice handled the matter like a lady. She didn't turn purple (as I would have done), neither did she open her purse, take out a gun and shoot her husband on the spot (as you might have done). She chose, in fact, not to discuss the matter at all. Unhappily Boswell decided that it was time for him to comment.

"If you take the queen of clubs," he said, "we hold it to three."

Alice rose from the table, went to the telephone and called her attorney who immediately filed for divorce. The case was recently heard by the Ontario Court of Appeal, whose decision was based on these two factors. What card was the worst one played? Who was to blame? Here are some excerpts from that landmark decision.

The Honorable Mr. Justice Pillowcase
For 20 years, ever since the World Championship of 1955, I've been pointing out, *ad nauseam*, that weak two-bids are no good, and this is just one more horrible example... If East hadn't opened two spades, who knows where it would have ended? I apportion 90% of the blame to East for her opening bid and 10% to West for agreeing to play the stupid convention.

Judge Mathe Mussels
I agree with my learned brother. The cause of the trouble was that pussy-footing preempt. Let East open four spades like a man instead of a Ms. and then we might have seen something. The worst card led? The spade four. I never lead partner's suit. Never!

Judge Elegant Troth
Divorce granted. What's the problem? No one had enough to open the bidding anyway. The hand should have been passed out.

Judge Howitzer Shrunken
The real cause of the calamity lies in the failure of the pair to use a forcing club system. Using a strong club you never get into any difficulty. This has been clearly shown in World Championship competition. In the old days when our players all used antiquated standard systems, we often came close to winning. Sometimes the decision remained in doubt right up to the last few hands. This resulted in a great deal of stress and strain on all the players. Since our boys have started using strong club systems we are generally wiped out after the first few boards, permitting everyone to finish the whole thing in a state of calm serenity.

Judge Roland Resulter
The worst card played was the ten of clubs. Had the declarer played the ace and king he would have dropped the queen and none of this would have happened. Don't think I'm resulting the hand. I've played the system all my life and I haven't lost to a doubleton queen in 15 years.

Verdict of the Court — Husbands and wives should avoid playing bridge as partners.

The second case was set out in a recent letter in the newspaper. It read as follows —

DEAR ABBY:

You hold three spades to the nine-spot, six hearts to the ace-king, four small diamonds and a void in clubs. Everyone is vulnerable and you open the bidding a weak two hearts. The next hand doubles and your partner bids three hearts. Right-hand opponent doubles, which is explained as being responsive, and it is your turn. You decide, in your wisdom, that the opponents are heading for a spade contract and it is time to set up the defense, so you make the clever lead-directing bid of four clubs. Much to your surprise everyone passes; and these are the four hands.

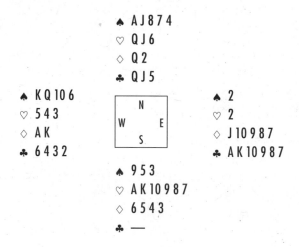

                ♠ A J 8 7 4
                ♡ Q J 6
                ◊ Q 2
                ♣ Q J 5

♠ K Q 10 6   ♠ 2
♡ 5 4 3   N   ♡ 2
◊ A K   W   E   ◊ J 10 9 8 7
♣ 6 4 3 2   S   ♣ A K 10 9 8 7

                ♠ 9 5 3
                ♡ A K 10 9 8 7
                ◊ 6 5 4 3
                ♣ —

The defense is sadistic. West opens a high diamond and shifts to a trump. He is put back in with a diamond and leads a second trump. All you get is two aces.

    This was a board-a-match team game, and at the other table your partners reach a contract of five clubs doubled. By playing the trump suit correctly, the contract is made by the declarer. When the time comes to compare scores he announces the result proudly, "Board 10, five clubs doubled making, plus 750." When I announce four clubs, not doubled, down eight, minus 800, he has a coronary right on the spot, and I understand is still in the hospital. That is not my main problem, however. My partner in this event was my boyfriend. We had been going sort of steady for some months and I was sure that he was just about ready to ask me a certain very important question. Ever since this hand, however, a certain coolness has crept up between us, and just last week I learned that he had asked Letty Lunkhead to play with him in the Mixed Pairs. Now Letty is nowhere the player I am, since she has not more than 40 masterpoints, while I am an Advanced Senior Master after less than six years of play. I can only presume that he is still angry about the harsh words that passed between us concerning this hand. Please, Dear Abby, you decide. Which of us was right and which of us was wrong, and how do you apportion the percentage of blame?

Yours sincerely,
AN ANXIOUS ADVANCED
SENIOR MASTER

DEAR ANXIOUS:

Your problem is indeed an interesting one. The whole subject of lead-directing bids has been ignored by most of our bridge authorities. It was necessary for me to refer to that Bible of Bidding, the *Bridge World* Master Solvers' Club. There the bid of a void or singleton to set up the defense has been proposed on several occasions. But even they have not discussed the more relevant point. Is such a bid forcing? That will have to be left for those more qualified than I to decide. After all, I am just a simple International Master.

There is a deeper psychological point involved, however. Just before you made your final bid, no doubt a look crept over your face, a look common to 90% of all bridge players in these situations. It was a look which said for all the world to see, "I am about to do something clever." Your partner's problem was really not what to bid, but how to interpret your cleverness. Were you being clever with a whole lot of hearts and a shortage of clubs, or were you being clever with a fistful of clubs and no hearts? The first would certainly be clever. The latter would be clever indeed. You gave your partner a 50-50 decision to make, and it is well known that in such cases partners will go wrong 75% of the time.

My earnest advice to you and to all bridge players, is this. Every time you feel the urge to do something clever, don't. It may not get you back your boyfriend. It will certainly improve your game.

Your Friend,
ABBY,
AN INTERNATIONAL MASTER

HOW I CHALLENGED THE CHAMPS AND MADE THEM CRY

> *"Challenge the Champs" runs in one form or another in almost every major bridge magazine. The format is simple: two pairs of experts bid a set of about ten hands, and are scored against each other based on their ability to reach the optimum contract in each case. Often the hands for the next issue are provided to readers, so they can try bidding them with their own partners. Of course, these are never easy hands, and routine bidding usually won't get you to the double-dummy spot. Michael Rosenberg provided a set of tongue-in-cheek rules for succeeding in these competitions in his autobiography* Bridge, Zia and Me. *Here's Frank Vine's take on the matter.*

This is in answer to the many requests from cronies and colleagues who have been clamoring for the secret of my success in "Challenge the Champs" competitions. Noting that my recent scores have all been in the low nineties, they ask, "How do you do it?" Here are a few of my golden rules.

Golden Rule Number One
Never open with a bid of one notrump.

You hold a nice 16- or 17-pointer. Evenly distributed, too. Are you about to bid one notrump? Then stop. Change your mind. You are headed for the ashcan.

The reason for this is quite obvious. It's printed right there on page one of every issue of *The Bridge World*: "Edgar Kaplan, Editor and Publisher; Jeff Rubens, Co-Editor." They are numbered among that small and dedicated group of desperate men whose mission it is to save the world of bridge: the Weak Notrumpers.

Now, a strong notrumper like me can be tolerant to a fault when it comes to the other fellow's bidding system. You want to use the weak notrump? All right, go ahead and use it; you don't bother me at all. But not the other way around. The weak notrumper is made of sterner stuff. He is a teacher, a prophet, and a missionary. It is his destiny to save us from the error of our ways, to line our pockets with gold or gold points at the tournament or rubber bridge table.

Witness his writings: "Here is yet another instance where the strong notrump failed to disclose the club fit leading to the cold minor-suit slam (on 21 points), which we easily arrived at when Larry opened the bidding one club on his doubleton queen," or, "Norman and I had great success with the weak notrump not vulnerable, but went down on every hand we opened with one notrump strong, when vulnerable." And so on, and so on. And remember, these are the people in charge of the store.

What to do with the strong balanced hand? The question to ask yourself is not what to open, but where is the hand headed. Certainly not to three notrump. That is never the right answer. What about four of a major? Not if you have to use the Stayman convention. Any fit you may uncover that way leads only to a disaster. Look instead for the cold minor-suit slam (on 21 points), or better still, the grand old 4-3 major-suit fit (another favorite of the Editors, which arouses even more hysteria than the weak notrump — but that's another story). Let me show you an example from real life.

November 1968, Deal 6

♠ J 3		♠ 10 8 7
♡ A K 6	N	♡ J 3
◇ A J 10 5	W E	◇ K Q 8 6 2
♣ K J 8 5	S	♣ Q 10 7

Both Eisenberg and Burger opened the West hand one notrump (like any normal human being), and, predictably, got to the wrong spot — Eisenberg to three notrump and Burger to three clubs.

Holding the West hand and following my theory, I knew that in any notrump contract the opponents were certain to run the first ten spades. Obviously, the par spot was either some number of hearts on the 4-3 fit, or else a minor-suit game, slam or partial. Accordingly, I directed my bidding to investigate these possibilities. The bidding went as follows:

Me: One heart (if partner should raise hearts, we are on our way).
Partner: One notrump ("I have not sufficient hearts, partner").
Me: Two diamonds (trotting out the next suit).
Partner: Three diamonds.
Me: Pass.

Score: Eisenberg-Goldman 2, Burger-Cayne 5, Vine and partner 10.

Suppose, you ask, it is your unthinking partner who picks up the balanced hand and bids one notrump? What then? This is also an easy situation to handle, if you remember that the auction one notrump-three notrump is *definitely out*.

July 1969, Deal 6

```
    ♠ A Q J                      ♠ 5 4
    ♡ K 8 4          N           ♡ A Q 10 3
    ◇ J 8        W       E       ◇ 7 6
    ♣ A J 10 9 7     S           ♣ K Q 6 4 2
```

Leventritt opened the West hand with one notrump and, after a Stayman investigation, settled in three notrump. Pabis-Ticci did better, getting to five clubs after his partner opened the East hand in first chair. I did better, of course, by following the corollary to Golden Rule Number One. When partner opened the West hand with one notrump, I automatically eliminated three notrump as a possible final contract. My opponents would obviously run a sickening number of diamonds or spades. Looking at the East hand, I could see that the destination had to be either four hearts (on the beloved 4-3), or five clubs. I investigated scientifically. To partner's one notrump, I replied three hearts. When he raised this to four hearts, that was that. Had he rebid three notrump, I would have given him five clubs. Simple? Simple.

Score: Leventritt–Crown 1, Pabis-Ticci–D'Alelio 7 (good bidders, those Italians; if they ever learn something about matchpoints they may go far), Vine and partner 10.

Golden Rule Number Two
You must never play in your long suit of seven or more cards.

The only problem with hands of this category is to get the contract played from the right side (usually your partner's), without bidding your suit. This is often easy to arrange, but once in a while you are required to think a bit in order to achieve the maximum result. After all, it is a contest. Thus:

May 1968, Deal 5

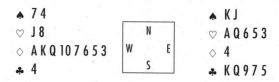

♠ 7 4
♡ J 8
◇ A K Q 10 7 6 5 3
♣ 4

♠ K J
♡ A Q 6 5 3
◇ 4
♣ K Q 9 7 5

Elliott, East, was the dealer and opened with one heart. Sheardown, West, unimaginatively responded in diamonds, and arrived at five diamonds. Fry, as West, more cunningly bid four notrump over his partner's heart opening, and when his partner replied five diamonds to the Blackwood query, he passed — the same contract, but from the right side. I held the West cards, and when my partner opened the bidding with one heart, using Golden Rule Number Two I automatically eliminated diamonds as a possible trump suit. The bareness of the other suits suggested that the contract should be notrump, but played from my partner's side. How to arrange this? Our auction went:

Partner: One heart.
Me: Three hearts (game-forcing).
Partner: Four notrump (Blackwood).
Me: Pass!

Score: Sheardown-Elliott 4, Fry-Koytchou 7, Vine and partner 10.

Golden Rule Number Three

When the opponents get into the bidding, your hand is good only when it is bad. The better it looks, the worse it will play. Moreover, you must never mention your long suit. Partner always has a void or singleton there.

The rule, therefore, is:

> *With a good hand over an opening bid by the opponents,*
> *look for the partial.*

April 1969, Deal 3

♠ A K J 9 6 5
♡ K Q J
◇ A 2
♣ 8 3

♠ 8
♡ 9 7 6 3 2
◇ 10 7 6
♣ K Q J 5

South opened the bidding with one club. Over the opening bid, Rank sensibly (he thought) jumped in his lovely spades to the two-level and played right there. Swanson mistakenly thought he held a good hand, and so he doubled the opening bid. When Walsh (East) responded one heart to the takeout double, Swanson drove to game in hearts. Both actions were unrealistic. Rank should have known that spades were out (suit too good), and Swanson that no hand this good could possibly produce game in a bidding contest. My auction was short and accurate.

> *South:* One club.
> *Me:* Double.
> *Partner:* Two hearts ("Surely, Mr. Walsh, the hand is worth this").
> *Me:* Pass!

Score: Rank-Crane 6, Walsh-Swanson 7, Vine and partner 10.

There are, of course, many more secrets available. If anyone should send me 25¢ and a self-addressed envelope, I just might (if I feel in the mood) forward my pamphlet entitled "More Tips on Beating the Champs."

NORTH OF THE MASTER SOLVERS' CLUB

Even more prevalent than "Challenge the Champs" in the world's bridge magazines is the feature The Bridge World enti- tles the "Master Solvers' Club". BRIDGE Magazine calls it "Marks and Comments" and the ACBL Bulletin "It's Your Call", but the format is much the same. An illustrious panel of experts is presented with a set of bidding problems, and asked to select a bid for each hand they are given, commenting on their choice. Perhaps the fascination in these affairs lies in the diversity of opinion that invariably attends every situation, with renowned experts adamantly insisting that their opposing views are the only sensible ones. Frank Vine, typically, had a unique perspec- tive on these matters…

We met in the smoky gloom of a little bar just down the street from the tournament. It was two o'clock in the morning, and I was looking for a friendly ear to bend. I spotted him sitting alone at a table in the corner. He was slight of build, slight of hair, harried looking. A good description for him was nondescript. And yet, I was sure I had seen him before. It must have been at the tournament. In the traditional American way, I plunked myself down at his table and introduced myself.

"I know you, don't I? You must be a bridge player."

For a moment, I was sure he was going to ignore me. He looked a bit frightened. Or was it wary? Then good manners prevailed.

"No, I'm not a bridge player."

That was not enough to stop me. "But I've seen you at the bridge tour- nament," I persisted. "I'll swear it. Wait a second. Now I've got it. You were kibitzing the knockout. And you were acting peculiar. During the bidding you watched like a hawk, but when the play began, you dozed off. I remem- ber thinking how strange that was."

He looked even warier. "I'm not much interested in anything except bidding," he explained. "That's my job. I work for *Bridge World* magazine."

He didn't look like anyone I knew. Then it came to me.

"No, no," he protested. "I'm not nearly that grand. I work in the Master Solvers' Club." That was even less credible unless one of the direc- tors had had a recent face lift.

"I think you're pulling my leg," I muttered belligerently. "You're not Rubens, you're certainly not Truscott, and as for Wolff…"

Again he interrupted. "I didn't say I was a director. I'm not. I'm North."

"You're who?"

"You know. North. A player you may have heard of, but one you have never sat down at the table with before. His bidding is neither too aggressive nor too conservative. You have had no chance to discuss your bidding system with him, so you are playing Bridge World Standard. All you know for certain is that he is an expert."

"Good Lord!" I exclaimed. "I never dreamt that you were a real person. I always took it for granted that the editors did the bidding."

"I'm real enough," he muttered wryly. "I've been on that job for more than thirty years."

I shook his hand warmly. "It's a pleasure to meet you. Imagine! Spending all your time bidding hands with the greatest players in the country. That must be paradise."

"Paradise!" He almost spat. "Purgatory is more like it. Those 'greatest players' you talk about — they have no consideration for anyone. Let alone a fellow expert."

"Come now," I protested. "You can't mean that."

"Can't I now? Just look at this hand.

♠ A742 ♡ K865 ◇ 92 ♣ AJ2

"Partner opens the bidding one club, and the next hand calls two diamonds. You make a negative double, of course, and partner leaps to four spades. It's your bid."

I pondered the situation. "I guess you could just blurt out six spades," I suggested. "But we might be off the first two diamonds. What about five spades? Doesn't that ask about diamonds?"

"It should. But to some it does, to others it doesn't. Remember, you're dealing with a polyglot group, many of whom have queer ideas on bidding. The only safe thing to do is *cuebid*. So you try five clubs. If partner bids five diamonds, six spades should be ice; even if he holds a singleton, or king and one, he may recognize the positional advantage and bid the slam himself."

"Wait a second," I protested. "Suppose partner thinks five clubs is a preference. He might just up and pass."

"If I were playing with a dodo, that would indeed be a problem. But, as you said, these are the best in the country. If all I had was clubs, I would have raised the first time. If I had hearts and clubs, I would have bid the hearts, and raised clubs later if necessary. But what I did was make a negative double. That always shows spades and hearts. Always! That's why partner jumped to four spades. Could he do that if he thought I might not have spades? Five clubs is a cuebid. That's called logic."

It certainly sounded logical to me. "What was the hand?" I asked.

"Just what you might expect. It was problem (B), *The Bridge World*, January, 1979:

♠ K Q J 6 ♡ Q 2 ◇ A 5 ♣ K Q 7 4 3

"As you can see, six spades is a fine contract."

"Perfect," I said. "As they're always saying in the Master Solvers', what's the problem?"

"The problem is that the majority of the panel *passed* five clubs. Not because they were dodos, but because they couldn't find it in their hearts to trust my bidding, even when they understood it."

"Come now," I soothed. "Surely that's just your imagination."

"Is it? Look at this comment from Ira Rubin: 'Pass. If partner is a bridge player he's making a slam try (to which I'd call five diamonds), but I'm afraid he's just another jerk with hearts and clubs.' Do you hear that? I'm the jerk. How do you like my job now?"

"Well," I pooh-poohed, "one isolated incident. You can't build a pyramid on that."

"Then try this one for size. It's from the issue of November, 1978. Problem (C). You hold:

♠ 3 ♡ 10 9 8 6 5 4 ◇ Q 9 7 ♣ A K 5

"Partner starts out with one spade; you say one notrump. Partner bids two diamonds; you respond with two hearts. Partner now bids three diamonds. Clearly, your minimum hand is very nice for partner. Even slam is a lively possibility. So what do you do? You bid *four clubs* of course! What else can it be but a cuebid? When partner says his hand is all spades and diamonds, only a cretin would keep on bidding new suits in the face of a misfit. I would expect a group of average players to know that much. But not our mighty experts. Holding this hand,

♠ A Q 9 6 4 ♡ 2 ◇ A K J 10 5 ♣ Q 5

cold for five or even six diamonds, twenty-two of them passed four clubs, and played in their three-two fit. Here is a typical analysis. *Hudecek* — 'If four clubs was some exotic super-support of diamonds… don't blame me.'

"*Director (Sheinwold)…* 'Fair enough. Just tell us whom we should blame?' I like that. For once a director came to my support. You don't get much of that these days. Have you noticed the change in style of directors? They're such nice guys, it's sickening. Now Morehead, he understood that thrust and counterthrust was the lifeblood of the contest. And Sheinwold. Remember how wonderfully he sliced people up? Today, no one even says boo."

"Perhaps it's time the experts were given their proper respect," I said.

"Bah! Proper respect. Why do they deserve respect? Give them a tough hand and they fall flat on their faces. Take this incident:

♠ Q J 7 ♡ A 8 3 ◇ A 7 6 4 ♣ A K 10

"This hand first came up as problem (F), *The Bridge World*, July, 1964. Albert Morehead had actually held the cards at the table. He opened one diamond, heard the next hand preempt four clubs, and, after two passes, it came back to him. He doubled. For penalties, is what he said. But his partner, thinking it was takeout, pulled to four diamonds. This was not a success. Morehead was so angry at what he considered his partner's stupidity that he took the case to the panel. When fifty out of sixty-three voted for double, he considered himself vindicated.

"A year later, Edgar Kaplan was guest conductor of the Master Solvers' Club. He had been brooding over this hand, and several others, for some time. Now he saw his chance to stick it to the panel. In *The Bridge World*, July, 1965, as problem (E), he introduced this hand…

♠ 10 9 5 3 ♡ 6 5 4 2 ◇ K 6 5 2 ♣ 3

The panel was given the auction: one diamond by partner, four-club overcall by opponent, pass, pass, and double by partner. As you may have guessed, this was the hand held by Morehead's partner the year before. What did the panel do? Forty-four out of forty-nine voted to pull the double! Most of them were the same geniuses who had made a penalty double with the other hand. And you call that bidding?"

"Calm down, now," I murmured. "You must remember that both Morehead and Moyse were men of strong opinions. Sometimes they went overboard." To my surprise my little guest became infuriated.

"Don't you dare say anything against Morehead or Moyse," he snarled. "At least they were fighters. We had some glorious battles in those days. Roth, Rubin and Kaplan attacking from the left. Rosler-Stern throwing spears. Oakie hacking away from the other direction. Mathe, Greene and Ehrlenbach fighting the good fight with us, shoulder to shoulder. It was glorious. Today the only excitement is when someone makes a bid out of turn."

Suddenly he looked at his watch. "Good Grief! It's almost three. I'll miss my train."

"Wait," I said. "I'd like to see you again and talk some more. Is that possible?"

He paused at the open door before disappearing into the night. "Anything is possible in the Master Solvers' Club."

WHAT'S THE PROBLEM?

I actually remember watching the Charlie Chan *TV series, which was popular when I was very young. Much of its appeal to viewers derived from Chan's mangled English and quaint "oriental" proverbs and similes. The series could never be made today, and even then raised some eyebrows by casting a Caucasian in the title role. However, the names Frank chose for this story, and its essential premise, commemorate another sleuth who had begun to make headlines just a few years before this was written:* Inspector Clouseau, of Pink Panther *fame.*

"It's not a problem, it's a catastrophe. Yesterday morning we learned that the computer hands for the upcoming Dogmeat Pairs, the most prestigious event in ACBL history, were microfilmed and sold. We have the signed confession of a trusted employee of the computer firm. We even know the identity of the thief, that notorious villain, the Lavender Leopard. He intends to enter the event and thereby gain sufficient points and prestige to start a lucrative business as a professional partner. I have been authorized by the Board of Governors to retain you, Inspector Clew Ho, the world's most illustrious oriental detective, to stop him. Can you help us?"

"Pardon ignorance of humble junior master," the portly Clew Ho replied. "Why not apprehend criminal when he buy entry, or in alternative, why not change the hands?"

"It's not that easy," I replied. "The Lavender Leopard is a life master of disguise. No one has ever seen his true face. As for changing the hands, the league refuses to give in to terrorism. The integrity of our computer is at stake."

"Humble detective will be honored to take case," said Clew Ho. "He and number-one son will be present at the game. Son will pose as caddy, Clew Ho as director. Together we will pluck the bitter fruit from the weed of crime."

For a while it looked as though we might all go home early. No sooner had the first session ended than Ho's number-one son ran into the scoring room. "Pop! Pop! I've got your man. Just look at this hand."

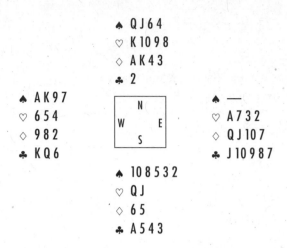

♠ Q J 6 4
♡ K 10 9 8
◇ A K 4 3
♣ 2

♠ A K 9 7   ♠ —
♡ 6 5 4   ♡ A 7 3 2
◇ 9 8 2   ◇ Q J 10 7
♣ K Q 6   ♣ J 10 9 8 7

♠ 10 8 5 3 2
♡ Q J
◇ 6 5
♣ A 5 4 3

The contract was four spades. The invariable lead (not best) was the king of clubs. Usually, South won his ace, ruffed a club, then played out the queen and jack of hearts to knock out the ace. East returned the queen of diamonds. Declarer threw a club on the king of hearts, cashed king of diamonds, ruffed a diamond, and ruffed his last club. Now he played a high spade. But West had three inevitable trump tricks. A few declarers won the club, ruffed a club, led a heart to the queen, ruffed a club, and led a heart to East's ace. In this variation, East returned a fourth club; West shed a red card. Once again, careful defense garnered three trump tricks.

At one table, however, South played differently. He won the club, ruffed a club, and forced out the ace of hearts, like most. But when he won the diamond return, he played the king of hearts and ruffed it! Then a club ruff, high diamond, diamond ruff. This was the position as he led his last club.

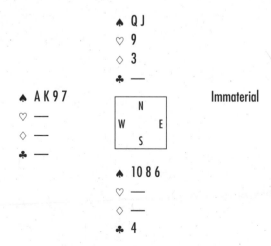

♠ Q J
♡ 9
◇ 3
♣ —

♠ A K 9 7   Immaterial
♡ —
◇ —
♣ —

♠ 10 8 6
♡ —
◇ —
♣ 4

"Whether West ruffs high or low, he is held to two tricks. No one would play like that, Pop, unless he knew the cards. He's our Mister Leopard."

"Hasty conclusion like poisoned mushrooms," said Ho. "Easy to swallow but hard to digest. What was bidding?"

"Standard, Pop. One club by West, double by North, a three-spade splinter by East, four spades by South, double by West."

"Astute declarer have advantage not of pre-knowledge," said Ho, "but of Eastern Scientific bidding. West play five-card majors and have only three clubs, since no sane partner jump in clubs without five. West cannot have four diamonds or would open bidding that suit; he have exactly three, since if East have five he still be bidding. Because of East's splinter, we know West have three spades at least; because of double, we find out he have four. That is why declarer is able to play hand like open book. Modern bidding like string bikini. Most revealing."

Session Two brought another flurry of excitement, and once again we thought we had our man. This time it was I who brought him to Clew Ho's attention. "Take a look at this hand," I said.

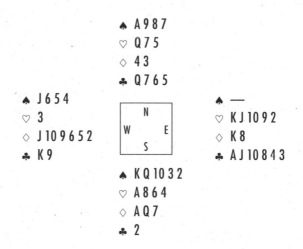

```
                    ♠ A 9 8 7
                    ♡ Q 7 5
                    ◇ 4 3
                    ♣ Q 7 6 5
  ♠ J 6 5 4                         ♠ —
  ♡ 3           ┌─────────┐         ♡ K J 10 9 2
  ◇ J 10 9 6 5 2 │    N    │         ◇ K 8
  ♣ K 9         │ W     E │         ♣ A J 10 8 4 3
                │    S    │
                └─────────┘
                    ♠ K Q 10 3 2
                    ♡ A 8 6 4
                    ◇ A Q 7
                    ♣ 2
```

Once again the contract is four spades. On the lead of king and another club, the declarer ruffs low, then cashes the king of trumps. After that, whatever he does he goes down one. That was the story at every table but one. Here, the declarer ruffed the club with his *ten* of spades, led a small trump and took an immediate finesse. Now came diamond to the queen, diamond ace, heart ace, second trump finesse, a club ruffed with the queen, a diamond ruff to dummy, and a club ruffed with the king. The ace of trumps was the tenth trick.

"There was a man who knew all the cards," I said.

"Excuse please," said Ho, "could noble ACBL President advise humble junior master of bidding at this table? Was same as at others?"

"Well, almost. But this was the only West who doubled the final contract."

"Aha!" said Ho. "Hungry doubler like matzo ball. Must end up in soup. No wonder declarer play double-dummy. What else can left-hand dummy hold except four trump to jack?"

The next three sessions passed without incident. The leaders in the event were all well-known experts, and we began to breathe again. Perhaps the Lavender Leopard had caught scent of our precautions and had decided to hunt elsewhere. Even Ho seemed to be losing interest; I noticed he was spending most of his time kibitzing that leading exponent of bidding theory, the renowned Alvin R. Much relieved, I went into the scoring room to relax. Fifteen minutes later my calm was shattered when a pale Alvin R. stumbled into the room prodded from behind by a revolver held by the great oriental detective.

"Clew Ho, are you mad? Do you know who that is?"

"Is one you are seeking. Lavender Leopard." He leaned forward, grabbed the nose of Alvin R. and deftly removed it. "Is not real Alvin R., is Leopard in disguise. Police are on way to attic in Utica where real Alvin R. held prisoner."

"Amazing, my dear Ho!" I exclaimed at dinner, later that evening. "How did you come to suspect him?"

"Elementary, my dear President. Suspicions aroused early when I pass table and hear his partner say, 'Sorry, I could have made that hand.' To which I hear Leopard reply, 'Don't apologize, you gave it a nice try.' That cannot be Alvin R., I say to myself, so I sit down to watch play. I see this hand.

♠ A Q 9 2
♡ 8 6 4 2
◇ A 10 3
♣ K 6

```
         N
    W         E
         S
```

♠ J 10 8 3
♡ A Q J 5
◇ K J 8
♣ A 3

"Contract was six hearts by Leopard, South. West led two of diamonds to ten, queen, king. Declarer played club to dummy and finesse heart. It worked. To get back to dummy for a second finesse, he led spade, to queen. Lost to king, and a diamond back — ruffed by West. Down one! To succeed, declarer must rise with ace of spades and take second heart finesse. It not possible declarer was Alvin R."

"See here," I protested, "I can't agree. The declarer has to be worried about a four-one trump break, and if that happens he needs the spade finesse for a slam. Surely, a bad trump break is a clearer and more present danger than the diamond being a singleton. In my opinion, he made the percentage play."

"Play was percentage but it not expert," said Ho. "Opening lead came like bullet. When defender leads quickly against slam, is it singleton or bottom of nothing? Real Alvin R. would have smelt singleton."

"Another thing puzzles me, Inspector. If the Leopard knew the hands in advance, how come he didn't know to refuse the spade finesse?"

"Ah so," said Ho. "Solution simple. I too have examined computer sheets. In bringing boards from next table to his, I remove king spades from West hand and place it with East. Fate is like fat man climbing mountain. Can always use helping hand."

At his trial the following year, the Lavender Leopard was found guilty of grand larceny, kidnapping and conspiracy to defraud. He was sentenced to five days in jail. For impersonating a bridge expert, the ACBL docked six masterpoints from his total. For tampering with a bridge hand, Inspector Clew Ho was barred from the ACBL for ten years.

There's a lesson there, somewhere.

THE ANNUAL BRIDGE AWARDS

One of Frank Vine's best pieces, this one received the ultimate accolade in 2008 when John Carruthers penned a sequel to it for The Bridge World — with full acknowledgment of the original, of course! The reference at the beginning is to the Omar Sharif Bridge Circus, which in the 1970s toured North America playing exhibition matches involving the Blue Team, the Aces, and local experts. For an insider's account of that fascinating venture, see Bobby Wolff's autobiography, The Lone Wolff, *or Omar Sharif's* Life in Bridge.

Can bridge become a spectator sport? Many insist the answer is yes. "What it needs is glamor," they say. So glamorous Omar arrives with his glamorous circus, and few are there to see.

"What it needs is drama," they say. So the reigning Blue Team comes to Las Vegas to deal with the young pretenders. Who is there to witness the titanic battle? Almost no one.

I'll tell you what bridge really needs. What it really needs is awards. Take all the successful audience producers. They have their Oscars and their Emmies. Their Tonys and their Edgars. The only thing equivalent in bridge is the McKenney Trophy race, and lately that has had about as much suspense as a Russian election. A select committee (my wife, my uncle and myself) has decided to remedy this situation. To proceed through regular channels would mean red tape and resistance. We have therefore taken it upon ourselves to present the first annual bridge merit awards, to be known hereafter as "The Moysies."

Presentation Number One

This deal arose in the Open Pairs event at a national tournament. At all 458 tables the contract was the same — six hearts, South to play.

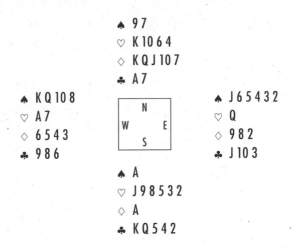

```
              ♠ 9 7
              ♡ K 10 6 4
              ◇ K Q J 10 7
              ♣ A 7
♠ K Q 10 8          N          ♠ J 6 5 4 3 2
♡ A 7                          ♡ Q
◇ 6 5 4 3       W       E      ◇ 9 8 2
♣ 9 8 6              S         ♣ J 10 3
              ♠ A
              ♡ J 9 8 5 3 2
              ◇ A
              ♣ K Q 5 4 2
```

The lead was the king of spades. Declarer won with the ace, put down the ace of diamonds, and led a small heart to dummy. Fearful that a spade loser was about to disappear on the diamonds, West rose with the ace of trumps. Curtains!

At all 458 tables, a discussion, sometimes amiable, often acrimonious, took place. Finally the question was put directly to the declarer. "What would you have done if West had played low on the first lead of trumps?" At 457 tables, the answer was the same. "I give you my solemn word. It made no difference what card you played. I had my line decided after the opening lead. I was going up with the king."

In Section Q, at table 6, the declarer was Calvin Sludge of Battle Creek, Utah. When the question was put to him, Calvin stunned his opponents and two eavesdroppers at the next table by replying, "I would have gone down one."

For his courage in casting a doubt on the perfection of his declarer play, for his candor in confessing to a lack of double-dummy hindsight, for admitting that he had cut down the cherry tree: To Calvin Sludge, of Battle Creek, we present the first annual "I Made Up My Mind at Trick Number One. Ifyoudaplayedlow, Idagoneup" Award.

Presentation Number Two

We have all been through the same experience. A bit of undisciplined bidding and you are in a contract that is at best touch-and-go — and an opponent leads out of turn. Is this heaven coming down on your side? Not on your life. If your experience has been the same as mine, you are about to be visited by a catastrophe.

The reason is mathematical. With the multitude of choices offered (e.g., accept the lead, bar it, penalty card, etc.) you are bound to be wrong more often than right. Nevertheless, the record of Elijah Grapefruit, set in 1954, of having guessed wrong ninety-eight times in one year seemed destined to last forever. To break this record would take a player of means and leisure, able to travel to a different Regional each weekend, and also one temperamentally suited to playing in the early morning games where a lead out of turn is the rule rather than the exception. It was indeed a thrill to see Grapefruit's hallowed record fall this year before the determined onslaught of Minnie Mincemeat of Dustville, Colorado. Moreover, Minnie's record-breaking bad choice was not one of your garden variety of wrong decisions, but a blooper of classic proportions, as all landmark decisions should be. This was the deal.

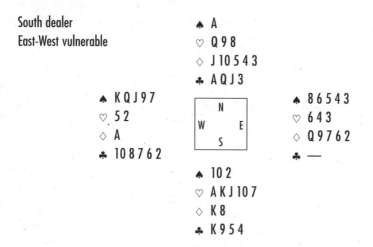

South dealer
East-West vulnerable

♠ A
♡ Q 9 8
♢ J 10 5 4 3
♣ A Q J 3

♠ K Q J 9 7
♡ 5 2
♢ A
♣ 10 8 7 6 2

N
W   E
S

♠ 8 6 5 4 3
♡ 6 4 3
♢ Q 9 7 6 2
♣ —

♠ 10 2
♡ A K J 10 7
♢ K 8
♣ K 9 5 4

WEST	NORTH	EAST	SOUTH
			1♡
1♠	2♢	pass	2♡
pass	4♡	4♠	pass
pass	5♡	all pass	

East led the eight of spades out of turn. Minnie considered her two apparent spade losers, and naturally barred the lead of the suit. West produced a small club. Ruff by East, diamond back; another club, another ruff; a diamond back, ruffed; a third club, a third ruff. Down three.

On a spade lead, declarer makes either five or six, depending on the guess in diamonds. To Minnie Mincemeat, we proudly present the first "With You for a Partner, Who Needs Enemies" Award.[1]

Presentation Number Three

Who made the bid of the year? As you can imagine, there were a host of sparkling contenders. Some were masterpieces of deep logic, others wild stabs that just happened to hit the target. The winning bid was neither of these. It was made by Stanley Cesspool of Chicago, in a game held at Deauville in Normandy. He was an American at his first French tournament. It was the wrong bid made at the wrong time by the wrong person for the wrong reasons. Naturally, it just had to be right.

Stanley was sitting East, holding the following cards

♠ 3 2 ♡ Q J 10 9 8 6 ◇ 9 3 ♣ 6 5 4

when LHO, the dealer, said, "*Un carreau.*" His partner, West, overcalled "*Un pique,*" North said "*Deux trèfles,*" and Stanley trotted out his best accent to say "*Je passe.*" Now South jumped to "*Trois carreaux,*" West said "*Je passe,*" North bid "*Quatre carreaux,*" and Stanley murmured "*Je passe*" again. South tried "*Cinq carreaux,*" West and North both said, "*Je passe,*" and now Stanley entered the auction with a firm "*Contre!*"

In plain English, this was how the bidding had proceeded:

WEST	NORTH	EAST	SOUTH
			1◇
1♠	2♣	pass	3◇
pass	4◇	pass	5◇
pass	pass	dbl!	

The double was followed by three passes, and this was the deal:

---

1. We commend to our readers Harry Goldwater's rule: "Always accept a lead out of turn. If he doesn't even know whose lead it is, what makes you think he knows what to lead?" — *The Bridge World.*

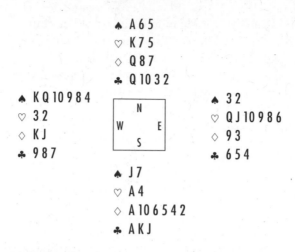

```
                    ♠ A 6 5
                    ♡ K 7 5
                    ◇ Q 8 7
                    ♣ Q 10 3 2
♠ K Q 10 9 8 4        ┌──────────┐        ♠ 3 2
♡ 3 2                 │    N     │        ♡ Q J 10 9 8 6
◇ K J              W  │          │  E     ◇ 9 3
♣ 9 8 7               │    S     │        ♣ 6 5 4
                      └──────────┘
                    ♠ J 7
                    ♡ A 4
                    ◇ A 10 6 5 4 2
                    ♣ A K J
```

West led the king of spades. Declarer won with the ace and studied the
dummy. Normal play, considering the few high cards out, is to play the vulnerable overcaller for everything: lay down the ace of trumps and lead small
towards the queen. As you can see, this would have produced five.

But what about the double? It could only mean that trumps were split-
ting badly. (What the double in fact meant was that Cesspool was having
difficulties with the French language. He thought that *carreaux* — diamonds — meant hearts — *coeurs* — and no one was pushing him around.
No sir! Not when he held six trumps to the queen-jack-ten. If they were
going to make five hearts, then they were going to make it doubled.)

Declarer played for the trump suit to be stacked on his right. He led the
seven from dummy and, when East played low, ran it. West won with the jack,
cashed a spade, and led a third spade. Declarer ruffed with a small diamond
(Stanley turned white), went to dummy with the king of hearts, and led the
queen of diamonds. When East played low again, declarer finessed. Down one.

The opponents were lavish with their praise. *Sacre bleu*! What a brilliant double! The declarer rose and kissed Cesspool on both cheeks.

Conscious that he was a representative of the ACBL in a strange land,
Stanley Cesspool did not let us down by confessing his error. He thanked
his opponents with quiet modesty and simply said, "In Chicago, monsieur,
we learn to bid 'em up."

To Mr. Cesspool, our congratulations and the award as "Bidder of the
Year."

Well, that's it for this year, folks. To the winners we extend congratulations. To the losers, we proffer this hope: "Don't lose heart. Maybe next year
you too can take home a Moysie."

CYRANO DE BLACKWOOD

The classic story of Cyrano de Bergerac has been retold many times, often successfully, as in the case of the movie Roxanne starring Steve Martin. The story of the man who helps his friend woo the girl he himself loves is timeless, and perhaps was a natural to be recast in a bridge setting.

Everyone liked him and nobody loved him. This did not bother Cyrano de Blackwood too much except in the case of the beautiful Roxanne, to whom his heart was irrevocably pledged, and to whom he never dared speak one word; for, as everybody knows, he was definitely unattractive, while she was definitely an ooh-la-la!

His bridge was good. He rarely came in first, but he never came in last. Everyone liked to play with him, for he was never cruel to his partner, never preached to his opponents, and never (well, almost never) resulted a hand. Who would have guessed that inside that nondescript exterior there was a great bridge expert screaming to get out? For Cyrano had only one bridge fault. Timing! After a hand was over, he could see, quite unaided, the brilliant stroke that would have turned this mundane deal into a work of art. If he could only compress the time it took him to *see* it into the time it took him to *do* it, he might be the greatest of them all.

Into this relatively unclouded life a bombshell fell, when he was approached by his handsome young friend, Christian de Dumdum, with this strange request.

"Cyrano, *mon cher*, you must come to my rescue. It is the fair Roxanne. I love her madly and I think she feels the same. Unhappily, in order to win that love, and knowing of her strange fascination for bridge, I exaggerated my past achievements. I will end up with quiche on my face unless you help me. Come to Lyons. I have arranged for an expert pair to be our partners in the knockout teams. Perhaps the genius of my partners will mask my lack of skill from her whom I adore."

Despite the pain in his heart, Cyrano agreed to help his friend, and the following week they were off to Lyons to compete for the *Coupe Richelieu*. Luckily, Roxanne was playing in the novice events, which were being held in a small inn on the other side of town, and would not be there to see. Later, of course, she would want to hear all about it.

The first match was hair-raising. Christian was not bad — he was awful. Cyrano, however, rose to new heights and that, combined with the expertise of their teammates, was enough to win. That night over coffee, Christian (as planned) pleaded a headache and retired to his room, leaving it to Cyrano to describe the day's adventures to Roxanne. He ended his recital with a hand he himself had played, pretending all the while that Christian was the protagonist.

South dealer
Both vulnerable

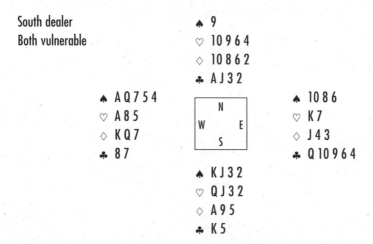

♠ 9
♡ 10 9 6 4
◇ 10 8 6 2
♣ A J 3 2

♠ A Q 7 5 4
♡ A 8 5
◇ K Q 7
♣ 8 7

♠ 10 8 6
♡ K 7
◇ J 4 3
♣ Q 10 9 6 4

♠ K J 3 2
♡ Q J 3 2
◇ A 9 5
♣ K 5

"Christian was South," began Cyrano, "and he started with a weak notrump. West doubled, and everyone passed. The opening lead was the five of spades, nine from dummy, the ten from East. It is the kind of hand where the important thing is not your score if you make it but your score if you go down.

"Most players would win the jack of spades and try a heart, playing for West to hold the ace-king or, more remotely, for East to have the ace of spades. As you can see, none of these nice things will happen. Instead, West will duck the first heart, hoping to get his partner in for a spade lead, and his partner will oblige."

Roxanne wrinkled her pretty brow. "But what else can declarer do?" she asked.

"He can do what Christian did," said Cyrano. "He can make his contract. This is accomplished by winning the opening lead, not with the jack but with the king! Now when the queen of hearts was led West went right up with the ace. If East held the king it would win a trick later. Right now, it was more important to lead a spade to his partner's known jack and have a diamond come through. When instead it was

Christian who won the jack of spades, there was a great silence in the enemy camp."

Roxanne clapped her hands in glee. "Oh, that Dumdum!" she sighed. "Is he not the greatest!?" Even Cyrano was happy. Although she did not know it, her delight was really in him.

The next day was scarier. The team they played was competent, and Christian was as bad as ever. Only the heroics of Cyrano and his teammates preserved a narrow win. That night, while Christian again stayed in his room Cyrano lied about the hands, ascribing the best of them to Christian. "Here is the one," he said, "that probably won the match."

♠ A Q J 9 8	N	♠ 10 7 4 3
♡ Q	W E	♡ J 9
◇ A 10 7	S	◇ Q J 9
♣ A 7 6 5		♣ K Q J 9

"Let us say you are West," he continued. "After South opens the bidding with two hearts (weak), you double and subsequently become the declarer in six spades. The opening lead is the three of hearts won with the king by South, who immediately puts down the king of diamonds. What do you do now?

"South cannot hold the king of spades. That would give him thirteen high-card points, and even a mouse would open that hand with a one bid. Is there any hope at all? Indeed there is. The diamond king appears to be a singleton. If South also holds three small spades, the play of the ace will drop a singleton king offside."

"Is that what happened?" asked Roxanne.

"Not quite," said Cyrano. "The declarer did play his ace of spades, but the king was doubleton... in the South hand! Christian had opened two hearts with the following:

♠ K 6 ♡ A K 7 6 4 2 ◇ K 8 4 ♣ 10 8

"As the opponents discovered too late, it takes a lion as well as a mouse to open such a hand with a weak two-bid."

Roxanne bordered on euphoria. "Surely," she exulted, "no one is more cunning than my Christian. I can hardly wait to see him and give him a big kiss." Poor Cyrano cringed inside.

The third day brought the reckoning. The team they faced was a good one, and Christian rose to the occasion and played his worst. They were also a slow team, so it was well into the night before they pulled out the cards for the penultimate hand. That was when Cyrano looked up and noted with distress that Roxanne had entered the playing room and had tiptoed to a kibitzer's seat just behind Christian. Luckily, it seemed to be a hand that even he could not abuse. The opponents, drunk with success, had pushed to three notrump on these cards, and on this auction:

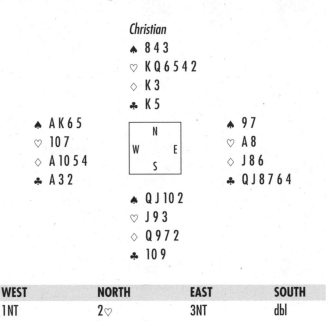

Christian
♠ 8 4 3
♡ K Q 6 5 4 2
♢ K 3
♣ K 5

♠ A K 6 5
♡ 10 7
♢ A 10 5 4
♣ A 3 2

♠ 9 7
♡ A 8
♢ J 8 6
♣ Q J 8 7 6 4

♠ Q J 10 2
♡ J 9 3
♢ Q 9 7 2
♣ 10 9

WEST	NORTH	EAST	SOUTH
1NT	2♡	3NT	dbl
all pass			

Christian led the king of hearts. The declarer ducked, Cyrano signaled with the nine, and Christian continued with the queen. Cyrano gritted his teeth and unblocked the jack. Now came the club finesse. Christian won his king and began to think. His ability to count was minimal and his ability to remember even smaller. The presence of his beloved, however, spurred him on to new heights. One heart was still out, and since the dummy had none and since his partner had been forced to drop the nine and jack, it must be in declarer's hand. Moreover, it was sure to outrank any of his small ones. Not being one to squander a high card when a lower one was available, he carefully led the two of hearts to his partner's three.

Cyrano was still in a state of shock when he picked up the next hand, which may explain why a conservative bidder opened the hand with one spade. After that, nothing could hold Christian back, and Cyrano found himself declarer at seven spades.

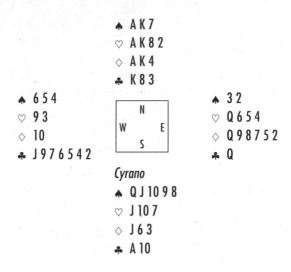

```
                    ♠ A K 7
                    ♡ A K 8 2
                    ◇ A K 4
                    ♣ K 8 3
  ♠ 6 5 4                              ♠ 3 2
  ♡ 9 3            ┌──── N ────┐       ♡ Q 6 5 4
  ◇ 10            W            E       ◇ Q 9 8 7 5 2
  ♣ J 9 7 6 5 4 2  └──── S ────┘       ♣ Q

                    Cyrano
                    ♠ Q J 10 9 8
                    ♡ J 10 7
                    ◇ J 6 3
                    ♣ A 10
```

West led a small club. Cyrano could see eleven tricks on top. Two more were available if hearts split evenly with the queen on side. Accordingly, Cyrano won the ace of clubs, drew trumps ending in his hand, and led the ten of clubs from his hand to try and get a count. When East showed out, declarer knew the heart suit was not behaving. The length as well as the queen rated to be with East. It was hopeless. At that precise moment, he chanced to glance up and saw Roxanne looking at him with shining eyes. To her, even to be present at the birth of a grand slam was ecstasy. She smiled at him, and that smile ignited a flame of inspiration. He played the ace of hearts, dropping the jack, and called for a small heart from dummy.

A lesser opponent might have played the queen, but East was experienced and had been there before. He saw that if his queen were ruffed the burden of protecting the heart suit would fall on his partner, who would be squeezed in hearts and clubs. Accordingly, he played low — and terrible things began to happen to him. Cyrano cashed the two high diamonds, ruffed a club to his hand and played out his last spade. East was forced to throw his queen of diamonds to keep two hearts, and Cyrano had the high jack of diamonds, the high heart, and his grand slam.

But it was not enough. His team still lost, and a disconsolate Cyrano was trudging to his room down the corridor of the inn when a breathless Roxanne caught up with him.

"Cyrano," she cried, "wait for me!" As he stood gazing dumbly with pounding heart, she said, "I know now that it was you and not Christian who made those brilliant plays that you described to me. You lied about him to spare my feelings. You are the noblest man I know."

Cyrano's heart beat wildly. "Does this mean that you and he are not getting married?"

Roxanne was astonished. "Of course we will get married," she said. "He is young and healthy and a productive earner. Those are the things that make a happy marriage. But you," she cried with fervor, "you shall always be my partner in the Mixed Pairs!"

THE MAN FROM LA MANCHA

Don Quixote would surely have been a bridge player had the game been invented in time. The idea of spending your time and money chasing something as fundamentally useless and ephemeral as "masterpoints" is nothing if not quixotic. Self-confidence is an important attribute of a winning player, and the Knight of the Doleful Countenance certainly had that in abundance. But it was the Latin poet Virgil who first wrote possunt quia posse videntur — "they can because they think they can". Watch as our heroine is inspired by her strange partner's vision...

She was a nice girl who played a bad game. She soon learned that a pleasant disposition could not compete with a bushel of masterpoints. People insisted on playing with their peers, and being at the bottom of the barrel, she had few partners to choose from. That is the way it was until the night of the Caledonia team championship, when those dramatic events occurred that started Dulcie Rumbleseat on her way to the top.

She arrived late, by design, hoping to find a place on some last minute pick-up team. As soon as she came in the door, the club director grabbed her arm.

"I've got a partner for you," he whispered, "It's that man over there. I've never seen him before. If you're willing to play, you can make up a team with Hazel and Hotspur."

He certainly looked weird. Lean, almost emaciated, a wispy van Dyck sprouting from his chin, the word that described him best was doleful. Except for his eyes. They burned and gleamed. "He looks a little mad," thought Dulcie, as she introduced herself.

"Aha!" he exclaimed. "'Tis Dulcinea. I have been waiting for you. At last the quest begins!" He bowed low over her hand. "My name is Don Keyhotay."

"The quest? What quest is that?" asked a puzzled Dulcie.

Her partner responded with passion. "To bid the unbiddable slam. To break the unbreakable hand. To beat the unbeatable foe. To restore the game to its ancient glory, when bridge was a duel of wits and not a clash of codes."

Dulcie decided that honesty was the best policy. "I'm not very good. I hope you won't be disappointed."

"Nonsense," said Keyhotay, "Dulcinea can never be anything but brilliant. However, since we have never played together, you may be a little nervous. Perhaps this will help." He handed her a small golden box shaped like a hat. "Behold the Golden Helmet of Mambrino. Whenever you are in distress, press the little button marked 'panic' and open the little box."

Distress arrived late in the match. Up until then the hands had been tame, and anything lost by Dulcie's timidity was compensated for by Keyhotay's swaggering play. Then came this deal.

East-West vulnerable
North dealer

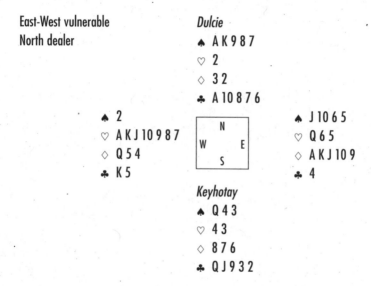

Dulcie
♠ A K 9 8 7
♡ 2
♢ 3 2
♣ A 10 8 7 6

♠ 2
♡ A K J 10 9 8 7
♢ Q 5 4
♣ K 5

♠ J 10 6 5
♡ Q 6 5
♢ A K J 10 9
♣ 4

Keyhotay
♠ Q 4 3
♡ 4 3
♢ 8 7 6
♣ Q J 9 3 2

Dulcie began with one club, East doubled, and Keyhotay raised to three clubs. West, a modernist in the grand tradition, decided that no number of hearts was right, and temporized with a cuebid of four clubs. Dulcie was in distress. She could raise clubs, introduce the spades, or pass. Her past experience told her that when she had several options she invariably chose the wrong one. It was time to open the Helmet of Mambrino. She pressed the little button, the top of the box flipped open, and out popped a little golden card on which these words were printed.

> "A little foolishness now and then
> Is relished by the wisest men."

That seemed clear enough. The trouble was that none of the options she had considered could be called foolish. In fact she could think of only one call that seemed to fit that description, so she chose it. "Four hearts," said Dulcie.

East passed, South corrected to five clubs, and now it was West who was in distress. If he bid five hearts that would be a cuebid and if he tried six hearts who knows what partner would do. So he decided to be practical and bid six notrump. Even Dulcie knew to double this and the resultant carnage was enough to win the match with ease.

So it was tied for the lead at the end of round one. Dulcie was thrilled but her partner stayed calm. "There is still," he warned, "a distance to go."

The next match found her facing the Hotshot brothers, two super-scientists whose specialty was confusing bids for confused opponents. The first hand was a prime example of their methods. Dulcie held the following

♠ 3 2
♡ Q 10 9 8
♢ A Q 8
♣ K J 9 4

and heard the bidding go as follows: two diamonds on her left (a weak two-bid in hearts or spades); two notrump artificial and enquiring on her right; three diamonds on her left showing an unspecified semi-solid major; three notrump on her right, to play. It was her lead.

The old Dulcie would have tried the three of spades. The new Dulcie took time out to open the golden Helmet. Out popped a second little card.

"When the bidding's polyglot
Lead the highest card you've got."

Following the instructions Dulcie put down her ace of diamonds. This was the whole layout:

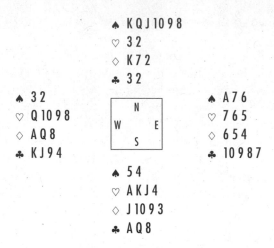

♠ K Q J 10 9 8
♡ 3 2
◇ K 7 2
♣ 3 2

♠ 3 2
♡ Q 10 9 8
◇ A Q 8
♣ K J 9 4

♠ A 7 6
♡ 7 6 5
◇ 6 5 4
♣ 10 9 8 7

♠ 5 4
♡ A K J 4
◇ J 10 9 3
♣ A Q 8

Dulcie followed up with the queen of diamonds and the declarer, unable to set up the spades, was held to eight tricks. At the other table the bidding was different but the contract the same. Here the opening lead was a pedestrian ten of hearts. After that, nine tricks were easy.

The result seemed to unnerve the Hotshot brothers and they quickly dissolved into slush as Dulcie and her partner trampled all over them. Two-thirds of the contest was over and Dulcie's team was still tied for the lead.

The excitement diminished when she saw whom it was she had to face next. It was Minnie Soda, nemesis of all the world's timid players, a corpulent menace who delighted in loud doubles of meek opponents. Dulcie revealed her fright to her partner.

"Ah yes," he said, "I have heard of her. The notorious Minnie Soda Fats. Possibly the brave Dulcinea can teach her a sharp lesson."

Dulcie doubted that, but putting on her bravest face, she advanced to the battle.

The first hand proved climactic. South was the dealer and this is how the bidding developed.

North-South vulnerable

Dealer South

```
              ♠ 10 8 4
              ♡ 10 4
              ◇ 8 7 6 3 2
              ♣ 9 5 4
  ♠ A K J                      ♠ 7 5 3
  ♡ K J 9 8        N           ♡ 7 6 5
  ◇ K Q 10     W     E         ◇ J 9 5 4
  ♣ J 10 7        S            ♣ K 3 2
              ♠ Q 9 6 2
              ♡ A Q 3 2
              ◇ A
              ♣ A Q 8 6
```

WEST	NORTH	EAST	SOUTH
			1♣
dbl	pass	1◇	1♠
2◇	pass	pass	dbl
pass	2♠	pass	pass
dbl!!	all pass		

Minnie led the ace of spades and although a continuation would have worked, she didn't feel like losing a trump trick and switched to a diamond. Dulcie won her ace and studied the situation. It didn't look good. Even if the king of clubs lay right *and* she could get to dummy *and* she could score her queen of spades, that was still two down. So she did what most players do in times of stress. She pushed the panic button. This was the message.

> Don't moan at your fate
> This isn't gin rummy,
> Remember my friend
> There's more than one dummy.

Actually that didn't seem too helpful, but Dulcie dutifully wrinkled her brow and thought and thought and finally got her first glimpse of expert light. She fired a low heart towards the ten.

Minnie took her jack and still reluctant to sacrifice a sure trump trick, returned a second diamond. Dulcie ruffed and again led a small heart towards the now singleton ten in dummy.

There is not the slightest doubt that it is right to rise with the king and play spades (just ask any resulter), but Minnie never dreamt that the ace of hearts lay anywhere but in her partner's hand, so she ducked with confidence.

It was all over. Dulcie finessed in clubs, cashed the ace, cashed the ace of hearts throwing a club, ruffed a club and ruffed a diamond to her hand, and that was eight tricks.

After that it was like taking candy from a baby. Minnie pitched IMPs all over the room and Dulcie and company were the new club champions.

Breaking away from a clutch of admirers, Dulcie looked for her partner. He had put on his cape and was already halfway out the door.

"Will we meet again?" asked Dulcie.

"I'm afraid the answer is no, my Dulcinea. I have many roads to travel and many battles to wage, and my time is running short. Tonight I am off to Toledo where I have scheduled a very important match against a windmill. Remember, however, the lesson you have learned. That the line between bad and excellent is a thin one, and the best way to cross it is to have as your partner someone who believes you have already done so."

A saddened Dulcie turned back to be overwhelmed by the congratulations of her friends. "Dulcie," they screamed, "you were marvelous. When can we have a game?"

"My name," she said. "is Dulcinea."

THE MOZART CONVENTION

In a story entitled "Everyone plays Zelig", David Silver parodied the Woody Allen film about a man who was part of every major event of his times, but was so nondescript, no-one could ever remember who he was. In the bridge version, the Zelig convention was universally adopted, but became known as Blackwood. Frank Vine's variation on the theme is of course based on Peter Shaffer's brilliant play "Amadeus", later an Oscar-winning motion picture. Curiously this story not only contains a reference to Blackwood but also to Stayman: the ultimate example of a convention becoming indelibly associated with a person who did not originate it.

He was once the toast of Vienna. Today he is just a footnote in the sands of time. He was a joy to play with. A cheery "Well done" when partner guessed right; a cheerful "Tough luck" whatever the blunder. These methods propelled him through the ranks of professional players until finally he had won, as his patron, Ferdinand himself, the Grand Duke.

You would think he had it made. But in his soul he was an unhappy man. Yes, he was the perfect partner, but what he really wanted to be was the perfect player. He tried, I'll give him that. He studied the masters, Reese, Simon, Kelsey, Marty Bergen. Every word was Holy Writ. He knew the story behind every great hand, but at the table something was lacking. When the chips were down, Saul E. Ari always struck out.

But never mind! In his heart he knew that if he stayed good, and studied hard, some day everything would jell. And then a worm entered the apple of his world.

It began innocently. One day the Duke mentioned that he was considering an addition to their knockout team. "A young player from the provinces," he said. "His name is Wolfie Mozart. I have invited him to our next practice match. We'll look him over."

Wolfie was not a success. First there was his appearance. A la mode for the young, his hair was long and dirty, his face unshaven, his clothing soiled and a bit pungent. Worst were his manners. A high-pitched cackle when someone erred, and an insulting remark to suit the occasion. This was the deal that cooked the golden goose.

South dealer
Neither vulnerable

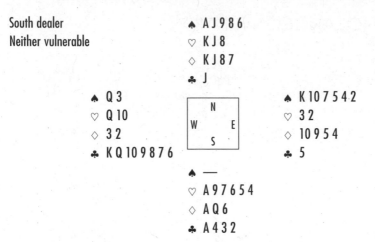

♠ A J 9 8 6
♡ K J 8
◇ K J 8 7
♣ J

♠ Q 3
♡ Q 10
◇ 3 2
♣ K Q 10 9 8 7 6

♠ K 10 7 5 4 2
♡ 3 2
◇ 10 9 5 4
♣ 5

♠ —
♡ A 9 7 6 5 4
◇ A Q 6
♣ A 4 3 2

In Ari's room, the auction started with one heart by South, and Ari, West, preempted three clubs. As often happens, this set the opponents off on a frenzy of overbidding, culminating in an unsound seven hearts. The lead was the king of clubs. South won, and led a trump: small, ten, king, small. It did not look promising. The ten was probably a singleton; declarer could pick up the queen, but that was only twelve tricks. He needed to ruff a club, but if he tried that maneuver East would overruff. So there was no choice but to play for trumps to be two-two. As you can see, that was how it was, and the grand slam rolled.

In the other room, with the Duke South, the bidding was the same, and Wolfie, West, also started the king of clubs. However, when a small heart was led Mozart tabled the *queen*. Now declarer had an option: he could ruff a club with the jack of trumps, then finesse East for the ten. It was probably the percentage play, and surely the classy one. But Mozart won the ten, and erupted with his imitation of a hyena and these famous last words: "This time it's *through* the iron duke, jerko."

That ended Wolfie's career as a high-priced pro. The word was out, and no one would hire him. Royalty had been irked. All he could pick up was the odd date at some small-town Sectional, usually with the wife of some *nouveau riche* wine merchant.

The result should have been pleasant for Saul E. Ari, but something gnawed at his bones. The play of the queen had not even entered his mind. Was there something missing in his make-up? Was it possible that a lout like Mozart could own the divine spark that he himself lacked, though more richly deserved? Where was justice? Or was it, after all, just a fluke play?

So he followed Wolfie's career. Playing with rotten partners, Mozart had no chance for glory. But now and then word leaked out of some spectacular coup, until, consumed by curiosity and fury, Saul E. Ari just had to see for himself. Learning that Mozart was entered in a Sectional in Liechtenstein, Ari arranged to attend. As luck had ordained, he faced Mozart on the first round.

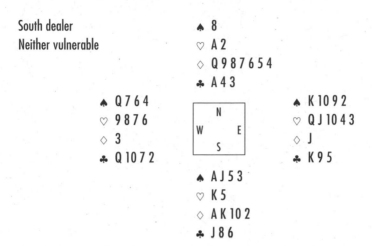

South dealer
Neither vulnerable

```
                    ♠ 8
                    ♡ A 2
                    ◇ Q 9 8 7 6 5 4
                    ♣ A 4 3
  ♠ Q 7 6 4                          ♠ K 10 9 2
  ♡ 9 8 7 6          N               ♡ Q J 10 4 3
  ◇ 3            W       E           ◇ J
  ♣ Q 10 7 2         S               ♣ K 9 5
                    ♠ A J 5 3
                    ♡ K 5
                    ◇ A K 10 2
                    ♣ J 8 6
```

Mozart, South, began with one diamond; North splintered with three spades, and Wolfie bid a quiet six diamonds. Saul E. Ari led his trump.

The legitimate play for the contract is to find either opponent with three spades to the king-queen or a doubleton high honor in clubs. Most good players would ruff a spade and, when no honor appeared, strip the hand; then ace and another club. That would, of course, be down one. Mozart went for the swindle. He won the trump lead in hand, and played a small spade to the eight. East won this with the nine; he returned a spade — small, small, ruff. Now all the trumps were played out, declarer pitching two small clubs. Then, ace and another heart.

On paper, this hand is easy to defend. In real life, three-card endings are treacherous animals. Are signals in the side suits count, or attitude? Or is partner being his usual brilliant deceptive self? The opponents could only be sure of one thing: declarer did not hold the ace of spades. So East came down to the king-spot of clubs, while West clutched his three clubs to the queen. This was not the way to do it. Mozart's cackle, and his "Thanks for the present, jerkos," did not make the result any easier to swallow.

The next deal was even harder to live with.

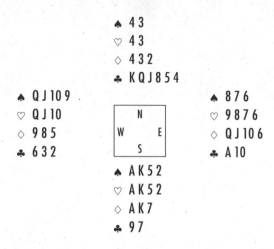

```
              ♠ 4 3
              ♡ 4 3
              ◇ 4 3 2
              ♣ K Q J 8 5 4
♠ Q J 10 9                    ♠ 8 7 6
♡ Q J 10          N           ♡ 9 8 7 6
◇ 9 8 5       W       E       ◇ Q J 10 6
♣ 6 3 2           S           ♣ A 10
              ♠ A K 5 2
              ♡ A K 5 2
              ◇ A K 7
              ♣ 9 7
```

Three notrump is not your most elegant spot but, really, it's hard to stay out of. That didn't bother Ari. Finally he recognized a situation from his extensive readings.

In 1957, writing about his success in the Life Master Individual (*The Bridge World*, March 1957), Edgar Kaplan had faced a similar problem. He had won the opening lead, and had pushed out the nine of clubs: small, king, ace. Winning the return, he led his last club. When West followed low, Kaplan inserted the eight, which held. His reasoning was impeccable. "My right-hand opponent was Norman Kay," he said. "Kay would never be guilty of an atrocity like winning the first club when he could kill the dummy playing low. Ergo, he must hold the singleton ace."

Similarly, Saul E. Ari led his club nine, and lost to the ace. He won the return, led his second club, and lost to the ten. Down three! Again the hyena cackle. "If you were playing against Norman Kay, jerko, you're only down two. You would have scored a club trick."

Ari returned to Vienna a man obsessed. He could not live in a world that contained Mozart. But how to do it? After several sleepless nights, he came up with a plan. The next day found him knocking at Mozart's door.

"Wolfie," he said, "I have come to make you a man of substance. I will pay you five hundred golden ducats if you will invent a convention, one that will bear my name. But no ordinary convention. A hundred years from now, like Stayman and Blackwood, the Saul E. Ari convention must be known to all. You make me immortal and I will make you rich."

Mozart grabbed the money, and promised immediate action. He was as good as his word. Two days later he was in Ari's drawing room, explaining. "Look at this hand," he said.

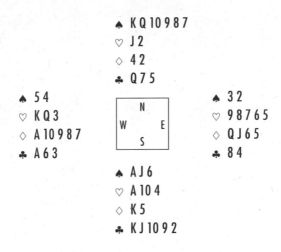

♠ K Q 10 9 8 7
♡ J 2
◇ 4 2
♣ Q 7 5

♠ 5 4
♡ K Q 3
◇ A 10 9 8 7
♣ A 6 3

♠ 3 2
♡ 9 8 7 6 5
◇ Q J 6 5
♣ 8 4

♠ A J 6
♡ A 10 4
◇ K 5
♣ K J 10 9 2

"You sit North. Partner is the dealer and opens one notrump. What is your choice? Two hearts transferring to spades, of course. The perfect contract has been reached. Four spades played by North goes down on a diamond lead, as does three notrump. Now suppose you, North, are the dealer. What do you open? A weak two spades no doubt. Now the only makable game is down the tube. Again, suppose West is the dealer and opens one diamond. What is your bid? A preemptive two spades? Pretty routine. But again you are doomed to play from the wrong side." Mozart's eyes were alive with excitement. "The answer is simple. Make all your preemptive bids transfers. Bid one below the agreed suit, and the strong hand is always able to declare." He fell back exhausted. "All this thinking has given me a headache. Have you got an aspirin?"

"Dear fellow," said Saul E. Ari, "I'll do better than that." Taking a glass of wine, he pressed a button on a large ring he wore on his hand. The top opened, and he poured out a healthy portion of a white powder into the goblet. "Swallow this," he said. "In one minute you won't feel a thing. I guarantee it."

The funeral of Mozart was hardly noticed. After all, who was he? Nonetheless, Ari waited several weeks before introducing the convention. A sensitive man, he was seeking the occasion. It came by way of a Regional in Salzburg, Mozart's home town. It seemed fitting to start there. Ari sat down with the Duke at a table facing well-known opponents. "By the way," he announced, "we'll be playing something new. All our preemptive bids are transfers."

"Oh," said an opponent, "you mean the Mozart convention. Everyone here plays that. He introduced it over a year ago."

"No!" screamed Ari. "Not the Mozart convention. He can't have it. It's mine. I paid for it." Screaming wildly, he was led from the room, never to be heard from in bridge circles again.

Today, he lives at a remote mental institution high in the Tibetan mountains. Once a month, there is a bridge game for the inmates, and every time it is Saul E. Ari's turn to bid, no matter what he holds, he makes a transfer preempt. Should anyone protest or criticize his bid, the response is always the same. A high pitched cackle followed by, "Who are you arguing with, jerko? I invented the bloody thing."

WEDNESDAY THE RABBI PLAYED BRIDGE

Anyone who was reading mystery novels in the 1970s will immediately recognize in the title of this piece an allusion to Harry Kemelman's series featuring Rabbi David Small and his congregation. The titles all involved days of the week: Sunday the Rabbi Stayed Home, Monday the Rabbi Took Off, *and so on. In the same way that Agatha Christie's Miss Marple was an unconventional sleuth, using her intimate knowledge of the people and mores of a small English village to help her solve crimes, the Rabbi juggled the politics and personalities of the Jewish community in a small New England town as he tracked down local malefactors. A rabbi is a scholar, a teacher and a community leader, not a priest, but David Small is a worthy descendant of G.K. Chesterton's Father Brown. I don't recall Kemelman's making any reference to the rabbi being a bridge player, but it would be an unusual synagogue without its weekly duplicate game...*

"So you see, Rabbi, we're in a pickle. Wednesday evening was supposed to be a happy time; a chance for wives and husbands to spend some time together at the synagogue playing bridge. The family that plays together prays together. I've heard you say that a hundred times." Marcus Needleman paused for breath. "Instead, there have been so many confrontations that already we have three couples filing for divorce, and I hear a few others are considering doing the same."

"That's tragic," said Rabbi David Pitzik, "but I don't see how I can help."

"The thing is, we need to establish a precedent. If you and your lovely wife Molly would come and play together next Wednesday, you could show the others how a proper couple behaves towards one other in times of stress. It would be of benefit to the whole congregation."

Rabbi Pitzik still demurred. "My wife is an experienced player, as you doubtless know, but I have not indulged since my Yeshiva days. What kind of an example would it be if your Rabbi made a fool of himself in public?"

"I really think you should come," said Needleman. "As president of the congregation, I must remind you that next Sunday is the annual membership meeting, and your contract is up for renewal. For a change there has been no shooting, strangulation, or other homicidal event involving a member for you to solve and thus earn everyone's gratitude. I think you should go to the game, and make every effort to win the dignity-and-decorum award, which we are handing out this week in place of the usual brilliancy prize."

As the good book says, better an untutored wage-earner than a hungry scholar, and the following Wednesday saw the Rabbi seated North at Table One facing, as his partner, his charming wife. He was committed to remaining cool, calm and objective, whatever the provocation. This resolve was instantly put to the test.

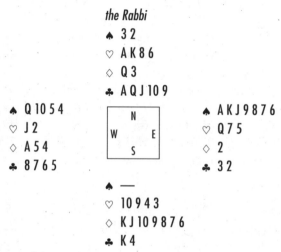

the Rabbi
- ♠ 3 2
- ♡ A K 8 6
- ◇ Q 3
- ♣ A Q J 10 9

West:
- ♠ Q 10 5 4
- ♡ J 2
- ◇ A 5 4
- ♣ 8 7 6 5

East:
- ♠ A K J 9 8 7 6
- ♡ Q 7 5
- ◇ 2
- ♣ 3 2

South:
- ♠ —
- ♡ 10 9 4 3
- ◇ K J 10 9 8 7 6
- ♣ K 4

The bidding started:

WEST	NORTH	EAST	SOUTH
	1♣	1♠	2◇
3♠	4♡	4♠	?

If you could see all the cards, the only slam you would want to be in is six diamonds. But how to get there in face of the enemy barrage? Considering her point count, Molly could have settled for five diamonds or five hearts without criticism, and the auction would surely have ended there. But she recognized the enormous playing potential of the hand, and gave it one more try. Five spades!

It was a challenging bid, and David rose to the occasion. Instead of an insipid six clubs, forcing Molly to take a blind stab, he correctly evaluated his diamond cards and came up with five notrump: "Pick your own slam, partner."

It was a first-rate effort. His partner found a third-rate response. Six hearts. David was nice about the whole thing. "We won't be alone dear. It's a trouble hand. And your five-spade bid was well conceived. Very few people will think of it."

Like many other people, Molly, a sensitive human being in almost every way, suffered from that peculiar psychosis that afflicts the bridge spouse — the compulsion to fall into a blind rage at anything resembling criticism.

"Well conceived, you dummy! Why, it was a brilliant bid. And the best you can come up with is to tell me you want to play the hand in notrump. And you don't even have a spade stopper!" Then, more sarcastically, "Or was that Blackwood asking for kings?"

The Rabbi kept his cool. "Remember what the Talmud says, my dear. Two wrongs don't make a right, but two rights may make a wrong."

"You want to know what the Talmud says?" she screamed. "I'll tell you what the Talmud says. Don't waste your best years on a klutz!"

This bit of wisdom seemed to satisfy her sense of justice, and the eager eavesdroppers did not have another chance for a few more rounds.

Dealer East
Both vulnerable

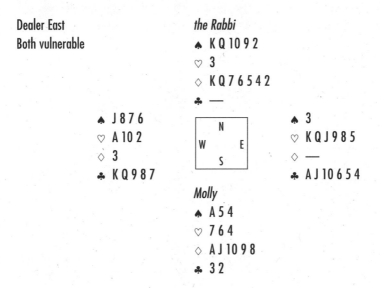

the Rabbi
♠ K Q 10 9 2
♡ 3
♢ K Q 7 6 5 4 2
♣ —

♠ J 8 7 6
♡ A 10 2
♢ 3
♣ K Q 9 8 7

♠ 3
♡ K Q J 9 8 5
♢ —
♣ A J 10 6 5 4

Molly
♠ A 5 4
♡ 7 6 4
♢ A J 10 9 8
♣ 3 2

It was a hand for strategic bidding.

WEST	NORTH	EAST	SOUTH
		1♡	pass
2♡	3♢	4♡	5♢
5♡	5♠	6♡	dbl
all pass			

Molly started out by leading the ace of spades. The Rabbi was in a quandary. A high spade would bring a second spade, and a low spade would probably beget a diamond. And what he desperately wanted was a club lead. Finally, he worked it out and played the king of spades, a startling move asking for a startling shift. But Molly stubbornly continued with a spade, and the slam was home. Once again the fireworks began.

"Did you have to signal such a high come-on?" she raged. "Didn't you want a club shift? Couldn't you play a small spade?"

The Rabbi was contrite. "I thought that if I did you might lead a diamond."

Molly stormed on. "Why would I lead a diamond? How can you want a diamond when I'm looking at the ace?"

David did not try to point out that he had no way of knowing what she was looking at, and remained firmly apologetic. "I'm sorry dear. I have this tendency to try to be clever, which is clearly contrary to biblical teachings — they tell us that the humble man does not try to illustrate his cleverness."

"What it should say," snarled his wife, "is that the humble man has good reason to be humble."

She felt better after that, and the expectant room returned to its own affairs.

Then came this problem in play.

Dealer South
North-South vulnerable

the Rabbi
♠ 10 4
♡ 5 4 2
◇ 5 3 2
♣ 10 9 8 4 2

```
        N
    W       E
        S
```

Molly
♠ A Q J 8
♡ A K Q J
◇ A K Q
♣ A Q

Molly, who fell in love with her hand, didn't stop bidding until she got to six notrump. The opening lead was the four of diamonds. Poor Molly! She could see no hope unless she could get to dummy to take a club finesse, and there was no way to get there unless the opponents blundered. And these particular opponents were only the best two players in the city. "Oh well, nothing ventured, nothing gained," she thought, and rattled off four hearts.

Everyone followed to three rounds, and on the thirteenth heart both opponents threw a diamond. Good! It looked as if it was safe to cash diamonds, so she proceeded to play the king and queen; and the suit broke. Now came a small spade to the ten, and West fell for it. He ducked his king. Molly had reached the dummy. Now, if there was any justice… She played the ten of clubs, put in the queen, and crossed her fingers. Alas, West won the king, and Molly still had to lose a spade.

The Rabbi, who had been watching all this with rapt attention, turned to his opponents in admiration. "That was, no doubt, a singleton king of clubs?" he asked. West admitted that it was.

"An exemplary defense," said David. "If left to her own devices, declarer will have no option but to play the ace of clubs, and will end up with her contract. You managed to give her a losing alternative. Brilliant!"

Molly was not filled with the same admiration. "You're not here to humiliate your partner and praise the enemy. Save that for the pulpit. No wonder I can't do better! I have three opponents instead of two."

David was immediately apologetic. "Forgive me my dear. I knew not what I did."

"The trouble is, you never do," she riposted. "And you can stick that in your Talmud and chew it."

The race for the decorum prize was no contest. The judges required only a moment's discussion before they called Rabbi Pitzik to the front of the room and awarded him a beautiful decanter filled with wine.

Rabbi Pitzik thanked them. "It is not by accident," he said, "that the Talmud declares that to find fault is destructive but to share the blame is unifying. And I might say further that without the help of my beloved wife I could not have won this lovely prize. Her constant nagging forced me to control my temper, and so in recognition of her contribution I shall share my honor with her." Saying this he went over to his wife and poured the bottle over her head.

The following Sunday, the congregation voted him a lifetime contract. Who says you can't win at bridge?

ANOTHER KIND OF BRIDGE DETECTIVE

> *Lieutenant Frank Columbo, played by the inimitable Peter Falk,
> was a fixture of 1970s television, and in many ways turned the
> TV mystery genre on its head. First there was the sleuth himself
> — slovenly, henpecked, forgetful, star-struck and even worship-
> ful of the Hollywood celebrities he was investigating, all this con-
> cealing a razor-sharp brain that worried away at the inconsis-
> tencies in the crime scene until he got at the truth. Then the
> murderer — he or she was usually a well-known actor, guest-
> starring for one episode. The show was never a whodunit; in
> fact, we usually saw the crime committed in some ingenious
> manner right at the start of each episode. The charm lay in
> watching as Columbo (in his scruffy raincoat and clutching a
> half-smoked cigar stub) gradually drew the net around the crim-
> inal, and in figuring out which tiny overlooked detail would trip
> up the murderer in the end. Time and again Columbo would
> come back, with his famous catch phrase, "Oh, just one more
> thing, sir — I almost forgot…"*

Last week, I murdered my wife.

Not that she was bad. Because she wasn't. In fact she was good, really
good. A warm, supportive human being. Except when she sat down at the
bridge table. Then, Dr. Jekyll turned into Mrs. Shrew: shrill, insulting and
malicious. Your typical bridge spouse. Last Wednesday the pot boiled over.
It was board thirteen (ironic, that) of the charity game at the Multicultural
Center, and I had just made a quite reasonable play that happened to turn
out badly. The ensuing eruption of invective continued unabated all
evening.

A proper gentleman, I refused to retaliate. However, the next afternoon
I brought the entire matter into the open.

"My dear," I began, "it is time we did something constructive about our
bridge future. The present situation just cannot be allowed to continue. It
demeans you and embarrasses me, one of the world's premier bridge players. No, we must cease playing together."

Despite my reasonable attitude, she was adamant, even spiteful. Not
only would we continue to be partners, but we'd be partners all the time
and not just on special occasions. So, you see, she left me no alternative. I

walked to the store on the corner, purchased a revolver and returned home and shot her three times in the head. After I had wrapped the weapon in plain, brown paper, addressed it to Cambodia and dropped it in the nearest mailbox, I drove to the club and waited for the authorities to arrive. I had managed several rubbers of Chicago before a police car finally pulled up. They delivered to me the shocking news that my wife had been murdered. They said that it appeared that my wife had startled some desperado in the act of theft. I had committed the perfect crime.

At least that is what I thought until two days ago. Again, I was playing a rubber at the club when a stranger sat down in one of the kibitzer chairs. I recognized him immediately. The mop of unkempt hair, the scraggly tie, the pointed, dusty shoes and especially the shabby raincoat, all were familiar to any serious watcher of television. Disguising my dismay, I wrenched my attention back to the game.

North-South vulnerable

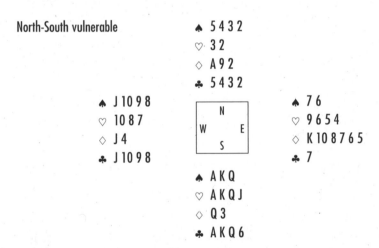

At six notrump, the lead was the jack of clubs. I played the ace, king and queen of that suit, and the same cards in the spade suit. Then came the four high hearts. On the queen I discarded a club from dummy, and on the jack West was trapped. He had to throw a small diamond. Now I produced the queen of diamonds, smothering the jack. East was skewered. If he took his king he would have to lead into the ace-nine tenace in dummy, and if he ducked I had my twelve tricks.

Following this display of grace under pressure, I rose from the table and my kibitzer took me aside. He immediately pulled out a worn wallet and showed me his badge.

"Homicide!" I exclaimed. "What do you want?"

"First of all," he said, "let me tell you how proud I am to meet you. I don't play much bridge myself, but my wife is one of your biggest fans. To tell you the truth, when it comes to bridge you are her god. Every time she reads the paper, the first thing she turns to is your column, even before she reads her horoscope. Wait until I tell her about that hand I just saw you play."

"Why did you want to see me?" I persisted.

"Well sir, I'm in charge of the investigation of your wife's murder, and there are a few small points that my superiors want me to clear up. Excuse me," he said as he tried to relight his cigar stub, "but did your wife have any enemies?"

"No," I replied.

"Well, did she have any bridge acquaintance who might want her out of the way?"

After I again answered in the negative, he rose, shook my hand briskly, and started to walk away. Of course, he got no farther than the door when he stopped suddenly, put his finger to his forehead, and spun around and scurried back.

"I almost forgot," he said. "There is one more thing. Does the nine of diamonds mean anything to you?"

"No," I said, managing to keep my face expressionless, "I don't believe so. Why?"

"Well you see, after your wife was shot she didn't lose consciousness right away. She managed to crawl to a table, pull out a deck of cards, and remove two of them. One was the deuce of diamonds; it was found three feet from her body. The other was the nine of diamonds; it was clutched in her hand."

"The nine of diamonds," I mused. "I think I may have it. The nine of diamonds is sometimes known as the 'Curse of Scotland.' Maybe she was trying to tell us that the murderer was a Scotsman, and the two of diamonds might mean that there were two of them."

He opened his notebook and began to write in it with a pencil. "The Curse of Scotland. Very good. Very, very good. Well, I guess that wraps it all up."

Again he shook my hand and again he left. But I knew we would meet again.

The next afternoon while I was in the midst of my thank-you address, having just been awarded the *BOLS* prize for the outstanding bridge tip of the decade, I was not surprised to notice his familiar figure slide into an empty seat in the back of the room. I was just completing my speech.

"And so," I concluded, "my advice to you, based on many years of experience in the field of battle, is this: When all the trumps are drawn, when there are no more losers, when all the rest of the tricks are yours, before you claim your contract *draw one more round of trumps.*"

I stepped down from the podium to thunderous applause and walked over to my tormentor.

"What is it now?" I demanded a bit peevishly.

As always, he was impossible to offend. "It's about that Curse of Scotland," he replied. "I spoke to my wife's brother. He's a very good player, a Senior Master, and he told me that the Curse of Scotland is the eight of diamonds, not the nine."

I shrugged my shoulders. "You can't expect me to remember all the spot cards."

He went on. "My brother-in-law also told me that if your wife was a good bridge player then those cards probably refer to some hand she played recently. Now I know that the two of you played bridge the night before the murder. Was there any hand in which the nine or deuce of diamonds was important?"

"Definitely not," I replied.

"Are you positive?"

"Lieutenant," I said, "a Life Master is always positive."

"Well, just to make sure," he said, "can you come with me to the Multicultural Center tomorrow afternoon just before game time and go over the hands? Maybe we'll find something."

That night, as soon as the clock struck twelve, I pulled on my navy-blue jeans, a dingy velour sweater, my dark glasses and a black beret and broke into the Multicultural Center. It was deserted.

I made my way to the games room and then to the tiny alcove where the boards are kept. Good, they were still there. With trembling fingers I removed the cards from the one I wanted and began to reshuffle them. The next moment, all the lights in the room went on!

The room was full of people, most of them police, and in the forefront stood my nemesis.

"It won't matter that you mixed the cards," he said. "I was here this afternoon with my brother-in-law and we went over all the hands. We figured it had to be Board Thirteen. Here, I've got a diagram," he continued, pulling out a sheet of paper.

Dealer West
Both sides vulnerable

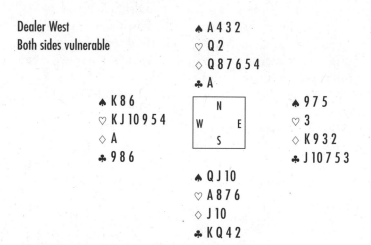

♠ A 4 3 2
♡ Q 2
◇ Q 8 7 6 5 4
♣ A

♠ K 8 6
♡ K J 10 9 5 4
◇ A
♣ 9 8 6

♠ 9 7 5
♡ 3
◇ K 9 3 2
♣ J 10 7 5 3

♠ Q J 10
♡ A 8 7 6
◇ J 10
♣ K Q 4 2

"Your wife sat West and opened the bidding with two hearts. North overcalled three diamonds and South went straight to three notrump. The
opening lead was the jack of hearts. The declarer won with his queen, and
led a diamond to his jack and your partner's ace. She continued with the
ten of hearts, and, when you showed out, the declarer took his ace and fired
back the ten of diamonds. You won with your king and correctly exited a
club. South now played the queen of diamonds, and you fell off your
pedestal.

"If you throw your nine under the queen, the declarer must go down.
He runs his diamonds but must let your partner in with a spade to cash her
good hearts. But you couldn't bring yourself to give up a good trick, and,
just as your wife tried to show us, you *threw* the deuce and *hung on* to the
nine. When South put you in with a diamond you were forced to lead a
black card, giving declarer the rest of the tricks. It was a bad play, and when
your wife complained, it cost her her life."

"Bad play! Bad play!" I chanted. "You sound just like her! How was I
to know that the declarer had misplayed his hand? Maybe he had the king
of spades and partner the king of clubs. Or maybe he had both black
kings. Then a discard of the high diamond hands him an overtrick or
his contract. The real reason for our zero was not my defense but North's
terrible bid of three diamonds. No one else made that crummy vulnerable overcall, and two hearts played by West was the contract at every other
table. But of course my wife couldn't accept that. All she could see was that

she had a bottom where she could have had a top. Because she was just like all the rest of the world, *another miserable resulter!*" I began screaming, "*Death to all resulters!*" as two sturdy policemen dragged me away.

The lieutenant just stood there shaking his head. "I guess he really is crazy," he muttered. "On the other hand, maybe he's just ahead of his time."

RASHOMON

It seems fitting to end this book on a high note, with what I personally think is Frank Vine's very best piece of writing. The 1950 motion picture Rashomon *is generally regarded as one of the finest films ever made. It is a Japanese crime drama with both philosophical and psychological overtones. An episode (rape and murder) in a forest is reported by four witnesses, each from their own point of view — and what each has seen is apparently very different. Who is telling the truth? Indeed, what is truth? Here a bridge crime is committed; we see it from the point of view of each of the protagonists in turn, and strangely, are led to ask the very same unanswerable questions...*

The Story as Told by the Warrior (West)...

Actually, I like to play with customers. Sometimes it's a real adventure. Take this interesting hand. We were vulnerable, they were not, and my partner opened in first chair with a bid of one diamond. The next hand said, "Skip bid — four hearts," and I found myself looking at this strange collection:

♠ A 10 4   ♡ A 10 2   ◇ A 10   ♣ A J 10 8 4

It is a truly tough problem, one that would tax the finest partnership. I could double (penalties) and would no doubt end up a little richer. But we were vulnerable, and a penalty would be false economy if a vulnerable slam lay in the cards. I could cuebid five hearts. That would get us somewhere. The trouble is, where?

I tried to visualize my partner's holding. No doubt, her hand was on the shapely side. Add four aces to a shapely hand and you most likely have a slam. Well, I certainly had the aces, and she certainly had the shape. But where was the slam? Then it came to me in a flash of inspiration.

I would bid Blackwood. She would, of course, respond five clubs, showing no aces. Then a bid of five notrump by me would guarantee all the aces. With that information she would be able to make an intelligent decision. I duly produced the master bid, four notrump. My left-hand opponent, a portly gentleman, passed quickly, and partner went into a long study. What the devil could she be thinking of? Finally she emerged with five spades!

What in blazes did five spades mean? I held four aces; she couldn't possibly hold three. I remembered the words of one of my confreres: "When you are playing with a customer, no matter how irrational his action, look for a reasonable explanation. Otherwise you will go out of your mind." So I thought and thought and finally saw the light. Partner held no aces, but she did have a void. Knowing that I must have more than one ace for my Blackwood bid, she was making the impossible call of five spades to alert me to her void. No doubt she held a hand something like this:

$$\spadesuit \text{K Q 6 5} \quad \heartsuit \text{—} \quad \diamond \text{K Q J 9 8} \quad \clubsuit \text{K Q 7 6}$$

My next call of five notrump, promising all the aces, would enable her to make the master bid of six hearts, after which I would call seven clubs, giving her a choice of grand slams. Hugging my elation to my breast, my face expressionless as usual, I bid five notrump. Again North passed, and again my partner went into a long huddle (who can blame her?). Finally her troubled brow smoothed out and she piped up with the unexpected call of seven clubs.

After my initial shock had passed, I gave a silent huzzah. My partner was not only beautiful, she was brainy. She had read my hand and the situation perfectly, and had come up with the winning call all by herself.

South gave this some consideration and doubled. I promptly redoubled to keep my partner from running. Alas, she finally fell from grace. I should have foreseen it. Unused to playing with such a fine partner, she had begun to doubt the wisdom of her previous bidding. In a state of total panic she ran to seven diamonds, and when this was doubled, to seven spades. Clearly we were now too high, and I made the marked conversion to seven notrump. We would go down, of course, but hopefully my partner would have learned something from the debacle...

The Story as Told by the Maiden (East)...

It all began at Christmas time, when Harold asked me what he could give a girl who already had a sable coat, a Rolls Royce, and a drawer full of rubies. I surprised him with my answer. "What I want, honeybun," I said, "is for you to buy me a bridge expert."

I had actually been thinking about it for a long time. A lot of my friends had bridge experts of their own, and some of them were doing very well indeed. I was just about the last person in the crowd who was not yet a Life Master. Harold was a little reluctant at first, but after he gave the matter some thought he told me to take my choice. That's how I ended up with this guy I was playing with in the Swiss Teams in the Peoria Fall Regional. He wasn't much to look at, and he wasn't the kind you would pick to go to the Spingold with; but he was supposed to be good for a few gold points every tournament, and that was what I was after. So far we had been getting along really well, and I had even brought home a couple of tough finesses, when this hand happened to me. I was vulnerable and they were not, and I held:

$$\spadesuit KQJ32 \ \heartsuit 4 \ \diamondsuit KQ65432 \ \clubsuit —$$

With my old partners I would either open three diamonds or maybe even pass, but my expert had just finished warning me about preempting in one suit when I held a four-card major, and this time I held a five-card one. I could pass, but he never likes it when I pass, so what could I do except bid one diamond? My partner would bid hearts or clubs, and then I could bid spades twice and he would know my whole hand. But the smart aleck on my left bid four hearts. Partner went into the longest huddle you ever saw. His face was twitching on both sides. I was just dying, because I knew that whatever he did I was going to be in deep trouble. Finally it came. Four notrump! What a relief — I knew what that meant. I had seen it in a bridge book just last week. One hand opened a club, an opponent overcalled four spades, and partner held:

$$\spadesuit 3 \ \heartsuit QJ987 \ \diamondsuit AKJ98 \ \clubsuit Q10$$

He bid four notrump. It was a takeout bid, asking partner to pick one of the other two suits. This was going to be easy. My partner had a good hand with clubs and spades, and I certainly had a preference. I could bid it right away, but I decided to make believe I was thinking for a while like all the big-time players do. Finally I came right out with it — five spades. Well, that certainly shook him. I could see that he hadn't expected me to be so smart. He thought for another long time and bid five notrump.

Well, that was another easy one. It was a grand-slam force, and I certainly had two of the top three honors. I was about to chirp seven spades when I remembered.

"When you hold two honors always bid seven clubs," he said, "otherwise you may be going against partner's intentions." So I bid seven clubs.

He would know what that meant. After all, I was paying him enough to know that much.

Obviously the smart aleck on my left didn't know what it meant, because he doubled.

"OK, wiseguy," I said to myself. "Let's see if you double my partner's seven spades." But partner didn't bid seven spades, he redoubled. I was certainly getting my money's worth on this hand. I guess he wanted me to make the master bid. Then I began to wonder. Was the master bid, in fact, seven spades? Maybe he meant diamonds all along. For the first time I had a teensy little doubt. After all, my diamonds were a lot longer. So I bid seven diamonds. South doubled this so fast that I knew it had to be spades. So I bid that, and partner spoiled it all by bidding seven notrump. I guess Rixi was right. All men are hand hogs...

The Story as Told by the Farmer (South)...

We were playing against this eyeful and her sourpuss partner, and everything had been going along pretty dandy when this hand came along:

♠ 9 8 7 ♡ K Q J 9 8 7 6 5 ◇ — ♣ K 3

The eyeful opened one diamond, and naturally I put it up to four hearts. Sourpuss not only waits the full ten seconds but takes another five hundred and forty before he comes out with four notrump. Naturally, he means he wants to play it there. (How else can you get to play in notrump?) But the female takes it as Blackwood (what can you expect?) and gives him three aces.

The lucky stiff, I think, partner makes a stupid bid and now you're going to come up smelling like a rose. But no. He still wants to play it in notrump. I can see he is all upset by her, because he grits his teeth and makes about a dozen different faces. Finally he comes out with five notrump.

The dummy still doesn't get the message because now she bids seven clubs! Holy cow, I think, they're in seven and vulnerable. I don't care how the idiots got there, I can't let them play if they're about to make. Luckily partner and I are playing this terrific convention called negative slam doubles. If you hold one defensive trick, you pass; and if you hold none, you double. Now partner knows whether to pull or leave the double in.

The question is, do I have a defensive trick? For sure my hearts don't mean a thing, they can't have a loser there. What about my king of clubs?

That's only good if I'm sitting over the ace. With my luck, the palooka has that one. I'd better follow the principle of insurance and show no defensive trick and leave the deciding up to partner. So I double, and the vulture on my left redoubles like a shot. "Oh, oh," I say to myself, "I just found the ace of clubs." Partner passes this, and blondie bids seven diamonds. Well if I didn't have a trick against seven clubs, I sure don't have one against seven diamonds; so I double again. This time the vulture passes fast (he likes it) and, would you believe it, the blonde panics and runs to seven spades. Well that's more like it. They might have been all right in the other suits, but no one finds a home at the seven-level in a suit they bid for the first time, not against me they don't. I'm going to belt this one for all the tea in China. This time it's the palooka who panics and goes to seven notrump. Would you believe it? Even my grandmother doubles this one. So I crack it and wait for my partner's heart lead. This one should be a real massacre…

The Story as Told by the Victim (North)…

If there is a moral to be learned from my story, it's this: Stay away from the partnership desk. If you need someone to play with, go out on the street and stop the first passerby. But stay away from the partnership desk. Just look at what happened to me. I held this miserable collection

♠ 6 5 ♡ 3 ◇ J 9 8 7 ♣ Q 9 7 6 5 2

and the bidding exploded on all sides. First my partner leaped to four hearts and then he doubled everything in sight. The final contract is seven notrump, and the final double sounds like it came from a wounded gorilla. Now it is up to me to find the lead.

Is there a clue from the bidding? I review the auction in my mind. Partner has doubled seven clubs, seven diamonds, and seven spades. Against all of these he would have been on lead. Ergo he must hold a cashable ace.

Which one is it? Can I tell from the bidding? Yes!

Since all club and spade bids by the opponents were clearly artificial, the only real suit they are known to have is diamonds, and the only ace my partner can have that is certain to cash is — you have it now — diamonds. With a feeling of triumph born of absolute confidence, I place the jack of diamonds on the table…

The rest is silence…

```
                    ♠ 6 5
                    ♡ 3
                    ◇ J 9 8 7
                    ♣ Q 9 7 6 5 2

♠ A 10 4                              ♠ K Q J 3 2
♡ A 10 2         ┌─────────┐         ♡ 4
◇ A 10           │    N    │         ◇ K Q 6 5 4 3 2
♣ A J 10 8 4     │ W     E │         ♣ —
                 │    S    │
                 └─────────┘
                    ♠ 9 8 7
                    ♡ K Q J 9 8 7 6 5
                    ◇ —
                    ♣ K 3
```

Master Point Press on the Internet

www.masterpointpress.com

Our main site, with information about our books and software, reviews and more.

www.masteringbridge.com

Our site for bridge teachers and students – free downloadable support material for our books, helpful articles, forums and more.

www.ebooksbridge.com (launching late 2008)

Purchase downloadable electronic versions of MPP books.

www.bridgeblogging.com

Read and comment on regular articles from MPP authors and other bridge notables.